"If you are looking to excel in any area of life or business, you must commit to mastering the fundamentals. *The Work before the Work* shows you how to do that at an elite level. Paul and Phil have done a masterful job creating the ultimate blueprint for sales professionals. Their combined experience and expertise are best-in-case, and this powerful resource is practical, applicable, and incredibly helpful. It is a must-read for any sales professional or business leader!"

ALAN STEIN JR., bestselling author of *Raise Your Game*

"Paul and Phil provide practical and proactive advice and pass on skills that differentiate the consistently successful sales professionals from those who struggle to achieve their goals. This book acts as a great reference for those serious about their development, and as a guide and template for what it takes to be up there with the best!"

ANT MORSE, head of innovation at Virgin Media O2

"There's no shortcut to success—you need to put in the effort. Paul and Phil give ambitious salespeople a comprehensive guide on how to incorporate the crucial elements of preparation before key sales activities. If you want to transform the outcome of your year and remain a cut above the rest, here's how to do it!"

BETHANY AYERS, COO at Peak

"WOW... just WOW! I've rarely seen such an important topic as sales preparation explained with such excellence. Sales teams executing the work before the work gain a fair advantage and position themselves as the vendor of choice, winning more deals in the process and gaining the immense gratitude of their many customers and clients whose businesses and lives are better off because of their work. If you're a sales manager or leader, be sure that every member of your sales team owns, reads, and uses this book. It's that important, and it's that good!"

BOB BURG, bestselling author of *The Go-Giver* series

"In their new book, Paul and Phil have laid it all out for you. Whether you're a true-blue sales professional wanting to get better at your craft or an entrepreneur with a desire to get better at selling in a smart, non-tacky manner, this is an absolute must-have addition to your bookshelf!"
CHRIS DUCKER, bestselling author of *Rise of the Youpreneur*

"In today's fast-paced environment, executives value new and credible ideas that accelerate their business towards desired outcomes. By carefully considering points of view and creating compelling perspectives, sales professionals can elevate themselves from seller to value contributor. In their new book, *The Work before the Work*, Paul and Phil outline a six-step framework that focuses on the preparation required for sales professionals to be able to offer indispensable insight and innovation in sales conversations again and again."
CONOR O'MALLEY, area vice president at Slack NEMEA

"To succeed in sales, you need to prepare. Successful sellers leave nothing to chance. *The Work before the Work* gives you access to tools through a great framework that will elevate you to the next level and help you become an even better seller. This is a great book to use as a navigation tool throughout your sales career. It's a must-read!"
HANNA LARSSON, start-up advisor and investor

"If you want to thrive selling products or services, get this book. *The Work before the Work* gives concrete, actionable guidance that will demystify what drives top-performing sales performance. Paul and Phil avoid gimmicks and instead give you the steps you can follow to get on the same side as your clients and potential clients while achieving remarkable results."
IAN ALTMAN, bestselling author of *Same Side Selling*

"What I appreciate about this book is that it proves there is no 'silver bullet' in sales. Instead of giving quick tips or shortcuts, Paul and Phil provide a solid framework that will drive results for anyone willing to put in the effort."
JOHN BARROWS, CEO of JBarrows Sales Training

"If you're working in sales or business development at a tech company like Salesforce, Google, Oracle, or Microsoft, then *The Work before the Work* is a must-read! So many aspects of the sales career, such as markets and territory, can be out of our control. This book breaks down the steps that we *do* control into play-by-play chunks so you can focus your concentration on making the most of *every* opportunity."
JOE FORGY, manager of business development reps at Salesforce

"If you are in sales and, like me, believe it is a much more complex career and role than the lazy stereotypes will have you believe, then I recommend reading this book. Without exception, those who succeed year after year are endlessly curious and do the work before the work. This book outlines a framework to help you ensure that you leave no stone unturned and deliver the results that make this job so rewarding."
JONATHAN HILL, regional vice president of High Tech at Salesforce

"Any sales executive, manager, or leader who strives to be a trusted advisor to their customers should explore this road map for sales success. Leveling up your pre-work will give you the confidence to improve your listening skills and more accurately uncover the pain and value that matters to your customers. Being well-prepared sets you apart from the competition; radiates curiosity, empathy, and authenticity; and primes your conversations for relevancy and action-able outcomes. This road map will first help you develop the trust required for your customer to agree to engage, and then help you build a mutual narrative for your solution value."
JULIAN MURRAY, sales director at Digital Asset

"While we've always known that hard work and how well you prepare contribute to consistent sales success, what Caffery and Jones have done is spell out exactly *what* that work is and *how* you go about doing it. Before you go sell what you need to sell, you need to read *The Work before the Work*."
LOU DIAMOND, bestselling author of *Speak Easy*

"*The Work before the Work* breaks down exactly what it takes to consistently perform at the top 1 percent level every single year, whether you are a sales professional or entrepreneur. Phil and Paul artfully break down how to win the game before the game even starts, with the core fundamental habits and belief systems of the elite. If you're truly serious about your craft and want to be world-class, this book is a must-read and will become your go-to bible for staying ahead of the game!"
MARCUS A. CHAN, founder of Venli Consulting Group

"One of the most relevant books on sale today, *The Work before the Work* is a compelling read that will have you turning pages and taking notes. Paul and Phil have not only written a book that captures the innovative and well-structured strategies that elite sales professionals use; they go one better and also show you how to integrate every strategy easily and effectively into your own sales process. A great read for every level of sales professional, guaranteed to deliver a strong return on investment."
MEREDITH POWELL, bestselling author of *Thrive: Strategies to Turn Uncertainty to Competitive Advantage*

"This holistic, definitive, and practical book is a powerful 'how-to prepare' guide for any sales professional and leader. Whether you're just starting out or have over twenty years' experience, this will help you reflect on and shape your approach for today's environment. The wealth of Paul's and Phil's experience shines throughout—they've mastered a fantastic balance of tactical, strategic, and practical advice to help you adopt an empathetic, customer-centric approach that will enable you to have meaningful, mutually beneficial conversations and outcomes, proven to drive consistent high performance. There are no tricks—only real-life use cases and sound practical advice. This is truly inspiring and refreshing. An absolute must-read!"
NATASHA DARCY SOUZA, Sales Excellence & Productivity EMEA, Google Cloud

"I asked my sales team to read this book and report back examples of its application. It was not long before the atmosphere in our weekly sales meetings became electric. The sheer empowerment each person felt by following the work before the work was tangible and infectious. Success breeds success. I really can't emphasize how important this book was in reinvigorating our sales team."

MICHAEL COTTER, founder of Wireless Connect

"Whether you're trying to transform lives and society or empower your company to win more business, or you're a salesperson aspiring to reach your potential, it's critical that your actions aren't built on sand. Over the last twenty years, I have seen that leaders who do the work before the work to create diverse and inclusive company cultures save money and win more—doing good at the same time. Paul and Phil's simple framework levels the playing field for everyone to gain a fair advantage and outperform their competition."

SANDRA HEALY, CEO and founder of Inclusio

"This book is a must-read for all sales professionals who understand that a sale begins long before walking into a room with prospects. It's the work you do beforehand that will allow you to leave an impactful first and lasting impression. Instantly demonstrating that you cared to prepare makes the difference between standing out or being average and between open doors or slammed-shut ones. Fortunately, being prepared is a skill you can learn. Paul and Phil's book comes with all the necessary insights and valuable guidance, plus a proven framework that makes it all easy to follow and impossible to fail, and sets you up for success."

SYLVIE DI GIUSTO, award-winning international keynote speaker

"Paul and Phil's book will help all those looking for guidance on how to give themselves the best chance leading into any sale. Preparation is key. Even seasoned pros need to rethink strategy sometimes, and the methodologies in this book will help you earn your prospects' trust from the outset and immediately increase your chances of closure. Having worked with Paul for many years, I can say there is no one better at being prepared, from the first call to closing. Paul Caffrey leads from the front, and it's evident from the very first page in this inspirational book."

TONY DI CARLO, cofounder and COO of Cloud Orca

"As someone who's read hundreds of sales books, I can say that so many are focused on the discipline required to be successful. What I appreciate about this book is that the focus is on the discipline of customer and prospect outcomes, not on the seller's own activities and metrics. This is what rebuilds and grows the mojo of the selling profession—and Paul and Phil have captured it here."

TODD CAPONI, bestselling author of *The Transparency Sale*

THE WORK
BEFORE
THE WORK

THE
WORK

PAUL M CAFFREY & PHIL M JONES

BEFORE THE WORK

The Hidden Habits
Elite Sales Professionals Use to
Outperform the Competition

PAGE TWO

Cataloguing in publication information is
available from Library and Archives Canada.
ISBN 978-1-77458-300-5 (paperback)
ISBN 978-1-77458-301-2 (ebook)

Page Two
pagetwo.com

Edited by Jenny Govier
Copyedited by Christine Lyseng Savage
Proofread by Steph VanderMeulen
Cover design by Peter Cocking
Interior design by Fiona Lee

paulcaffrey.com
philmjones.com
boxoftricksbooks.com

Camila, te amo, more than words . . .
Você é o mundo para mim.

Amelie and Marina—my inspiration,
my purpose, my sunshine, my everything!

PAUL

In loving memory of
Michael Caffrey.

Contents

1

Opening Words

Phil M. Jones

HAVE YOU ever wondered why some sales professionals have the ability to consistently win year after year, yet others have peaks and valleys or fail to reach their true potential?

With my experience working with over two million sales professionals globally, spanning almost every industry and sector—from the smallest of solopreneur businesses to some of the world's biggest brands—it has become crystal clear to me how elite performers maintain their consistent levels of success.

Sure, it's true that hard work, dedicated effort, product knowledge, an attractive personality, and even knowing *Exactly What to Say* can all have compounding positive impacts on your success in sales. But the factors that contribute to long-term and consistent success are perhaps a little more than that. The challenge is that almost all who have reached this insane level of competence have done so over time, through experience, and have organically evolved into their current self, so perhaps even they themselves fail to identify the attributes and components that have allowed them to repeatedly gain a fair advantage over their competition.

This book was imagined following a discussion that my coauthor, Paul, and I had about the modern sales professional and how the common stereotype of being pushy, slimy, dishonest, aggressive, and annoying could not be further from the truth of what we have experienced of those at the very top of their game. By contrast, our experience of elite performers has been that they do a number of things very differently from the stereotype. Almost without exception, they have a process, consistent habits, and high levels of emotional intelligence; they are people of high integrity; and they operate with intense levels of curiosity. Their mindset is fueled by strategic optimism and a relentless discipline that allows them to show up properly prepared for the moments that matter in their day. They know with complete certainty that their success is entirely dependent on the creation of successful outcomes for their customers and prospects, and they perform a series of non-negotiable habits that can all be encapsulated under a simple and profound heading: The Work before the Work. The reason I refer to these as non-negotiable habits is that these professionals never *don't* do this work.

In a world full of books by people trying to sell you on a shortcut to elevate your personal performance, this book is very different. You will find approximately zero "hacks" and not a single "trick," and at no point will you discover a hidden "secret." Instead you'll discover the meticulous thinking, questioning, and preparing that the best of the best unconsciously practice, which results in them outperforming their competition before the competition has even gotten started.

We've distilled this into six "hidden" habits: questions most people don't ask, but that elite sales professionals use again and again, and which you can incorporate into a preparation ritual. Think of it as a road map to allow you to gain a fair advantage in almost every selling situation, kind of like having the ability to start a soccer match with a three-goal advantage, a tennis match already one set up, or a marathon at the eight-mile marker. Doing the work before the work will deliver you success when prospecting, selling, and looking for your next promotion.

We almost titled the book *Exactly How to Think*, because what you are about to experience is a framework for your thinking. The book is delivered in two parts that are expertly guided by Paul and his vast practical experience of personifying *The Work before the Work* in his career: The first part (chapters 3 to 5) focuses on a series of questions to help you think about exactly *what* you can achieve, and the second (chapters 7 to 9) consists of a series of questions to help you think about exactly *how* you can achieve it.

Between these two parts, you'll hear from me again with some strategic input that will further heighten your effectiveness when engaging with others. The framework presented is designed so that whether you have merely moments to prepare or you are developing a long-term strategic approach, the action of committing time to think before you act is always respected.

As you work through the chapters, you will be prompted to think about the needs of all parties holistically. This is shaped by applying three purposeful lenses:

- Your customers' wants/needs
- Your personal wants/needs
- Other key stakeholders' wants/needs

Thinking through these three lenses will allow you to naturally heighten your empathy for all involved before you take a single action. In the business of deal-making, creating environments in which everybody wins is always the utopian outcome.

Speaking of outcomes, I am guessing that one of your desired outcomes from this book is to learn more about the framework I have been talking about and start to apply it to your own unique circumstances. So with that said, it's time for Paul to share with you what you'll need to know to incorporate the strategies in The Work before the Work into your work.

Essential Companion Downloads

The Work before the Work assessments and worksheets are available at paulcaffrey.com/work.

Elite sales professionals ritualize professional preparation and practice it every day. You can download our professional preparation templates for prospecting, selling, and getting promoted as often as you need.

CHAPTER SUMMARY

- Elite salespeople have habits, processes, and the relentless discipline to show up properly prepared for the moments that matter in their day.

- Preparation can be an innate ability or an acquired skill.

- Insanely competent sales professionals perform a series of non-negotiable habits to be ready for opportunities; they never *don't* do this work.

- Any sales professional can incorporate the six "hidden" habits into their own preparation for prospecting, selling, and getting promoted.

- Sales preparation requires you to know exactly *what* you have the ability to influence, and then plan exactly *how* you can achieve that outcome.

- Get essential companion downloads at paulcaffrey.com/work.

2

The Work *before* the Work before the Work

Paul M. Caffrey

Definition of "the work before the work":

a ritual of professional preparation that gives sales professionals a fair advantage.

PAUL M. CAFFREY

F TWO tennis players of similar age, ability, and experience are playing a match and one puts time in to prepare but the other doesn't, what is likely to happen? The match will be close, but more often than not, the player who prepared will win. Why? Small margins make a significant difference. Imagine that the prepared player studied their opponent and discovered they are unable to generate power returning weak serves aimed at their backhand, and their recent play close to the net has also been a little off. Imagine that this player then arranged a training session with a similar opponent and asked them to mimic the strengths and weaknesses of the player they were preparing to face. The prepared player will be match sharp, and when those critical points in the game come along, they will be better equipped to win them due to their preparation.

In sales, we don't get the luxury of witnessing exactly what our competitor is doing with the prospect, and sometimes we are competing with more than one other company for the business. Elite sales professionals don't rely just on their experience to get them through a sales meeting or even a full sales cycle but also on professional preparation. Some prepare instinctually, while others have a preparation process. Most sales professionals don't prepare adequately for sales activities because they don't have a process, and most don't consider the impact that preparation has on the outcome.

In this book we will show you how to ritualize your sales preparation. First, we will explain how to instantly prepare yourself for unexpected encounters with prospects, customers, and leaders who can influence your career. Then we will show you six habits you can use in tactical preparation for prospecting activities, like cold outreach and qualification calls; sales activities, such as meetings and running sales cycles; and promotion activities, including networking with leadership and navigating interviews. We will also cover strategic preparation for long-term plans and goals. For tactical and strategic opportunities, you will schedule time in your calendar and do the preparation, and apply instant preparation in all other situations. We recommend that as you start to apply these preparation habits, you make notes at the end of each day on how your sessions went. Be honest with yourself and admit where preparation was done, where it wasn't, and what wins you got from being prepared that day. Taking the time to prepare for the sales activities and noting the outcome on a daily basis are habits that will dramatically increase your success.

Keep an Open Mind and Be Willing to Take Action

Before we embark on this journey of professional preparation, how open-minded are you to increasing your sales performance this year? How open-minded are you to getting the most from this book?

I want you to think of three sales professionals, entrepreneurs, or executives you know. Could they benefit from finding and closing more business? Do they have knowledge they could share that would help you? Can you tell them that you are about to read this book and you will let them know your thoughts when you finish it? Then ask them for a recommendation of the best business or sales book they've ever read. This is an unusual request, but all will become clear toward the end of this book. We truly believe in the power of professional preparation and want to help as many like-minded people as possible. Most people won't do this, but elite sales professionals will because they believe in the value of a great professional network and know that random correspondence can produce serendipitous opportunities that one cannot imagine! Now extend your arm back fully—and throw that boomerang as hard as you can!

We strongly believe in the law of reciprocity and the power of taking action. Taking this particular action is the first measure of how successful you will be with the habits we share in *The Work before the Work*. Why actually do this? Simple. There are thousands of great books with great ideas. More often than you might expect, you will receive a recommendation of another great sales book, possibly one in a niche you never expected. This will open your mind to even more great sales ideas outside of this book and make you even better at selling! When you get a message back, share the books that are recommended to you for a secret bonus at paulcaffrey.com/bonus.

Your Preparation Assessment

Ever wondered how ready you are for a prospecting call, a sales meeting, or even the year ahead? Most people rely on intuition—either they feel ready or they do not. Professional preparation will always be subjective, but you can assess your preparedness now at paulcaffrey.com/work.

The R.E.A.D.Y Ritual

More often than not, elite sales professionals are ready for the opportunities that come their way because they prepare, come hell or high water. We all have habits and rituals we do every day—like brushing our teeth; starting the day with a hot coffee; and checking email, the news, and social media on our phone—and then we have habits and rituals we do from time to time. On holidays we wear sunscreen; we might read a couple of times a week when we get the chance, and we find time to meet friends every so often. The danger is that you will agree with this book, get excited and apply the power of professional preparation over the next couple of weeks, and then forget about it and go back to your usual preparation routine. As mentioned above, we will be inviting you to take an assessment to help you get started. Throughout the book we want you to seriously consider where professional preparation fits into your life and the positive impact it will have on your current situation.

When an opportunity comes your way, no matter how big or small, ask yourself: *Am I ready?* To make it easier to turn professional preparation into a daily habit, we use the R.E.A.D.Y. method:

Review Your Calendar.
Establish the Preparation Level for Upcoming Calendar Commitments.
Add Preparation Time to Your Calendar.
Do the Preparation!
You're Ready.

R: Review Your Calendar

At the start of your workday, review the meetings booked for that day and the next. At the end of your workday, review the meetings booked for the next two working days—it's likely the next day will have slightly changed. Diarized commitments might range from prospecting tasks to sales meetings or even opportunities to network with influential people who can help your career. Elite sales professionals list the meetings that are important and require preparation.

E: Establish the Preparation Level Required for Upcoming Calendar Commitments

Once you have decided what meetings and sessions you must prepare for, you need to establish the level of preparation required. There are three levels of professional preparation: instant, tactical, and strategic. We will delve into each in more detail shortly, but for now, consider instant preparation as two questions you ask yourself when you meet someone unexpectedly or when you have a meeting in your calendar that's of low importance. The majority of professional preparation for elite sales professionals is tactical preparation, which will have some preparation time scheduled. Meetings and opportunities that will have a major impact on your success this year are given strategic preparation. The professional preparation matrix, which we share a little later in this chapter, will help you decide the level of preparation to apply.

A: Add Preparation Time to Your Calendar

The amount of time to schedule for preparation will vary, but a great guide is to schedule fifteen to thirty minutes for tactical preparation and one to two hours for strategic preparation. Instant preparation can be completed just a couple of minutes in advance or when you meet someone unexpectedly. Add the preparation to your calendar as an event, and you can even change the calendar event color to make it stand out.

D: Do the Preparation!

This is the hard part—actually doing the preparation. Nobody will call you out if you haven't done the work before the work. A couple of seconds into the meeting, you will know if you're prepared or not, and it will be immediately obvious to the person you are meeting too. The more sales professionals do the work before the work, the higher the chance of a successful outcome.

Y: You're R.E.A.D.Y.

Reviewed your calendar at the start of the day? Reviewed your calendar at the end of the day? Established the level of preparation required? Scheduled the preparation? Done the preparation? Good news: you're now ready!

Connect Professional Preparation to Something You Do Every Day

To improve the likelihood of you actually bringing professional preparation into your sales routine, it's best to tie it to something you do already. Since our days are generally based on calls and meetings, which live on our calendar, the calendar is the best place for the R.E.A.D.Y. ritual. Adding the R.E.A.D.Y. ritual to your calendar for five minutes at the beginning and end of the day is a logical next step. It can be a stretch, but just before you log off for the day, checking your calendar and applying this ritual will make you much more likely to succeed.

The Three Levels of Preparation

Instant Preparation

Sometimes you just don't get the time you need to prepare for a sales activity, customer meeting, or serendipitous encounter, be it in person or virtual. A customer might call you unexpectedly, your prospect might add someone else you weren't expecting to a virtual call, or you might have a chance meeting with someone who can open doors for selling opportunities or even for your career. What most people don't realize is that you can prepare for those moments in seconds by asking yourself: What is this person looking to achieve? And how are they going to achieve it? Once you answer that, quickly ask yourself the same questions: What am I looking to achieve? How am I going to achieve this? This takes seconds to do, and it's a hidden habit of sales professionals that can be used in any part of life. This miniscule level of preparation will put value at the heart of your conversations and increase the likelihood of more positive outcomes more often. People are wired to want to pay back what they receive in social situations. This increases the chances of you giving them value, which increases the chances of them giving you value too.

If you bring this level of instant preparation to all your daily interactions—be they chats with internal peers, scheduled calls with customers, prospecting, or random conversations at networking events (virtual or in person)—then you will have a much better chance of finding that customer with a large project that you can turn into a large deal. Even if you're limited to the prospects you can speak with, it can be a great way to navigate a large company too. Instant preparation turns some fleeting conversations into lasting relationships, transforming conversations from interesting idea exchanges into worthwhile value exchanges.

Tactical Preparation

When the outcome of a situation is more impactful and we have a little more time to prepare, tactical preparation is the default approach to use. This is carefully planned preparation to gain a fair advantage in a competitive situation. Time available and the impact of the activities will determine how much time to spend on preparation. Important activities such as qualification calls, sales meetings, and even networking with hiring leaders deserve tactical preparation because you are in a competitive situation and working toward impactful outcomes.

When you have an initial sales call in your calendar, you can prepare tactically by applying the six hidden habits of elite sales professionals. Let's imagine we have a qualification call scheduled with a chief operating officer. We want to be clear on what we are looking to achieve together.

First let's consider the prospect's perspective. What is the COO looking to achieve? From notes and research, we speculate it's to increase the efficiency of the operations team's manual processes. The COO is the decision maker but requires the team's buy-in too. How is the COO going to achieve the desired outcome? The notes suggest the COO is thinking that the way forward is a number of point solutions that address individual challenges. Experience suggests the COO may focus on key features instead of the impact of the desired outcome. Extra guidance on the importance of the outcome may be required, along with agreed measures of success. This will need to be confirmed with the prospect. Then consider the six questions for other influential stakeholders—this is particularly relevant for the decision-making process and for measuring success.

Now let's consider what we want to achieve. What is the current situation, and what is the decision-making process? From the notes we receive and our research, we decide we want to qualify the COO's requirements and get them to agree to an evaluation; we want to confirm what they are doing today and why they want to change (and why now?); and if it appears that the coo has final say and sign-off on the project, we want to confirm that they have sole decision-making power or understand who else needs to be involved. We then ask ourselves how we are going to achieve this. Well, research is useful, but perhaps we plan specific questions to ask, prepare a couple of slides to give a visual representation of a sales evaluation, and use it as an opportunity to get more people involved on the customer's side. Then we ask ourselves how we are going to progress the desired outcome, which could be a shared plan for the evaluation and high-level agreement on the call to book the next few sessions into our calendars. How will we measure success? We could decide to measure whether the customer completes the evaluation and how fast. This is useful because over time, we can determine how effective our qualification calls are.

Because this preparation is tactical and you are in a competitive situation, you will have more success if you determine who the competition is at an early stage in the deal.

As you can imagine, being this thorough with your preparation will enable you to progress deals faster because you will sooner find the hidden challenges you'll need to overcome. It does not matter what sales process you follow: tactical preparation accelerates you from one step in the sales cycle to the next. Don't worry; we will go into more detail on this throughout the book, and there are companion downloads to guide you.

As The Work before the Work is a thinking framework, sometimes you will consider the six preparatory questions in a tactical situation and realize you should think strategically about one particular question to get a better outcome. We will cover how to think strategically for all situations so that you can use the framework in more detail when required.

Strategic Preparation

Those who apply strategic preparation to long-term goals, overall aims, and anything that will have a high impact on their success over the course of the year are more likely to achieve the best outcome. Strategic planning for the organization is the responsibility of leadership, and strategic planning for your sales success is your responsibility. Strategic preparation is the means by which to gain an overall or long-term fair advantage. Since the stakes are higher, with a bigger outcome to play for, the preparation is more in-depth, to give you a greater chance of success.

Sales activities that deserve strategic preparation include prospecting campaigns, annual sales attainment plans, the sales cycle for larger deals, and your campaign for promotion. When these activities are successful, their outcomes will have an immense impact on your success for the year. Successful prospecting campaigns mean more leads to work; more successful sales cycles mean more closed business; and a successful promotion campaign means a better job. All of these activities will cause you to earn more money.

So where does tactical preparation end and strategic preparation begin? This means going deeper into each of the six hidden habits of sales preparation. Let's take the first question: What are you looking to achieve? We apply this to ourselves, the people we deal with directly, and any other potential stakeholders. Stepping into strategic preparation means working through specific scenarios, such as the best possible outcomes for the people you're targeting, for yourself, and for all other stakeholders, as well as the broad possible outcomes and the career progression opportunities. As you work through the book, you will dig into the strategic preparation in a similar way for each of the hidden habits.

The outcome of strategic preparation is a readiness that makes it much easier to achieve your biggest goals for the year. You can never be certain of the outcome, but you will have a greater chance of certainty when it comes to achieving your goals this year if you can master the practice of preparation.

The Nine Core Activities for Prospecting, Selling, and Getting Promoted

If you're like me, when you read or listen to books, you can't wait to put the knowledge into practice to start getting results. To make this process a little easier, we will run the hidden habits through three areas that all top sales professionals practice regularly: prospecting, selling, and getting promoted. The good news is that you don't need to change how you prospect or sell in order to benefit. You will simply apply a series of questions—a thinking framework—to the activities you already do. These questions give you the power of professional preparation, which will make each sales activity more impactful and outcome oriented. They will also improve how you transition through the sales process, making it a better experience for you and your customers.

Some people will be more focused on prospecting and others on improving their selling abilities, or perhaps going for a new role, which makes focusing on getting promoted more appealing. What area will you improve? All three? The aim is to ritualize these habits and make them your own, so pick and choose the aspects of this book that make sense for you to apply. It's not the people who read this book who will become elite sales professionals; it's the people who apply the hidden habits day to day, week to week, month to month. Even if you just apply the tiny hidden habit of instant preparation, you will see a dramatic improvement across the board.

Each chapter will provide questions to ask yourself when preparing for the nine activities outlined in the following table:

Prospecting	Sales	Getting Promoted
Prospecting Campaign (Strategic Preparation)	Sales Attainment Plan (Strategic Preparation)	Campaign for Promotion (Strategic Preparation)
Qualification Calls (Tactical Preparation)	Sales Cycle (Tactical Preparation)	Interview (Tactical Preparation)
Cold Outreach (Tactical Preparation)	Sales Meetings (Tactical Preparation)	Networking (Tactical Preparation)

Figure 1: The Most Common Activities for Sales Professionals

In the area of prospecting, we will focus on three key activities: cold outreach to prospects, qualification calls, and running a prospecting campaign. Each chapter will provide questions and examples based on these activities. The hidden habits will amplify your prospecting results. From the sales perspective, we will focus on a sales meeting with a customer or prospect, running a sales cycle, and your annual sales attainment plan to exceed your target. The hidden habits will improve how you sell and increase your close rates. Finally, we will cover how you can advance your career by honing your skills when networking with hiring leaders, doing interviews, and running a campaign to gain promotion.

It's fascinating that many salespeople are suppressed by thinking that elite sales professionals have a veneer of excellence that allows them to operate above others, as if they possess superpowers. The superpowers—or, to be more specific, the hidden habits they possess—are available to all people at all levels.

Our challenge to you is to consider the prospecting, selling, and career progression opportunities you have coming up, whether or not they are in your calendar, and start thinking about how the techniques in this book can be applied to those commitments. Consider your goals for the year and apply the thinking framework to them. Each chapter spotlights hidden habits you can use today, so each time you pick up this book, choose one of these habits and apply it! Sometimes a gentle reminder to do something small is all we need to do something that turns out huge.

The Six Hidden Habits

Now that we are clear on the nine activities we will apply this thinking framework to, let's dig into the simple structure of the thinking framework itself. Each hidden habit is posed in the form of a question to think about. For each question, there are three scenarios to run through, and in most cases, there are three stakeholders to consider: them (whether that's a prospect, a customer, or a hiring leader), you, and everyone else (key stakeholders). The bigger the outcome you're working toward, the deeper you'll go with the preparation.

Choose what parts of the framework to apply and it becomes remarkably easy to use. This framework helps you to go from selling to people to earning the right to make a recommendation. It powers your ability to come across as credible and curious and to go deeper to get a better outcome.

Here are the six questions that reflect the hidden habits of elite sales professionals:

- What are you looking to achieve?
- What is the current situation?
- What is the decision-making process?
- How are you going to achieve this?
- How will you progress the desired outcome?
- How will you measure success?

How Much Preparation Is Needed?

If you are meeting an existing customer virtually and it's just a short conversation, you might think about the upcoming call and quickly ask yourself these six questions. However, for high-value outcomes, you'll delve deeper into each hidden habit. For instance, perhaps you have a first meeting with a prospect for a potentially valuable piece of new business. Let's take the first question—what are you looking to achieve? We run this through three scenarios:

- What's the best possible outcome to achieve?
- What are the broad possible outcomes that can be achieved?
- What career progression can be achieved?

When considering each scenario, look at it through three lenses: that of the person or business you're meeting, yourself, and other key stakeholders who have influence on your objective. For strategic preparation, you will go through a similar process for each habit. This thinking framework will power your professional preparation to help you gain clarity on the best possible outcomes and the considered action required to achieve them.

The amount of preparation you should do depends on the impact of the activity. As we discussed, there are three approaches to professional preparation to choose from: instant, tactical, and strategic. For instant preparation, ask yourself two questions: What are you looking to achieve, and how will you achieve it? For tactical preparation, you will ask six questions. It's the third approach, strategic preparation, that delves deeper into the nuances of each habit. To make it easier to decide how much effort to put into preparation, the following matrix will guide you:

	Optimal Preparation Time Available	Minimal Preparation Time Available
High Impact Activity	**Strategic Preparation**	**Tactical Preparation**
Low Impact Activity	**Tactical Preparation**	**Instant Preparation**

Figure 2: *Professional Preparation Matrix*

Even if you have just thirty seconds to prepare, you can gain clarity on what outcomes you and others need to achieve. Considering this will give your conversation more purpose and make it more impactful.

If you have a low-impact activity with a lot of time to prepare, then running through the six questions of tactical preparation—the questions that reflect the six hidden habits of elite sales professionals—will be more than adequate. The preparation you choose may vary depending on the circumstances and the number of opportunities you work on annually. For you, for example, a qualification call could be either a low-impact or high-impact activity. How do you decide? Well, how many qualification calls will you get the opportunity to host in a year? Some sales professionals might have multiple qualification calls per day, in which case the outcome of the qualification call is of low impact. On the other hand, if you're in enterprise sales, perhaps you get to have a qualification call only once a quarter. This then becomes a high-impact activity, since it could have a dramatic impact on your sales performance. In the Professional Preparation Matrix (see page 25), we've assigned specific levels of preparation to the various activities, but you should adjust the amount of preparation you do according to your own circumstances. In the chapters that follow, we've provided examples of questions you could consider when doing strategic preparation, no matter the activity.

For a high-impact activity with limited time or a low-impact activity with adequate time, running through the six questions mentally before the activity starts is recommended. For better results, consider the other party's aspirations and everyone else's too. In both scenarios, even just fifteen minutes of preparation will make a world of difference. The more you practice the art of professional preparation, the more success you will have.

If you have a high-impact activity planned with optimal time to prepare, this is the holy grail, and it should be put into the calendar as a non-negotiable activity. The more you prepare, the easier it becomes. Running through the six hidden habits, applying the three situations for each question, and ensuring you consider the viewpoint through the three lenses of the other person, yourself, and everyone else involved will be invaluable. It will help you see the gaps in your approach, give you clarity of outcome, and reduce your chances of missing something that is needed at a later point to get a deal done.

To use the framework effectively, create your Professional Preparation Matrix, pick the appropriate quadrant (depending on the impact and time available to prepare), and make it the cornerstone of your preparation. Whether you have a couple of seconds or a couple of months, you can apply the art of professional preparation to outperform your competition.

Go to paulcaffrey.com/work to get a copy of the Professional Preparation Matrix.

CHAPTER SUMMARY

- Consistent preparation gives sales professionals a fair advantage over their competition.

- Connect the habit of scheduling preparation to something you do every day.

- As for preparation for unexpected meetings, consider: What is this person looking to achieve, and how are they going to achieve it? Ask yourself the same questions.

Questions to consider in advance for those you meet and yourself:

- What are you looking to achieve?
- What is the current situation?
- What is the decision-making process?
- How will you achieve what's required?
- How will you progress the desired outcome?
- How will you measure success for all parties?

3

HIDDEN HABIT #1

What Are You Looking to Achieve?

Paul M. Caffrey

The start of becoming successful is **to truly define the word in your own terms.**

PHIL M. JONES

BEST POSSIBLE *outcome? Broad possible outcomes? Career progression?*

Elite salespeople know what they want to achieve for the year, the month, and even the day. So many talented salespeople aren't clear on what they want to achieve, but they know what they *need* to achieve. Their focus is on scrambling to make a target instead of being firmly set on exceeding the target. It's advisable to know what prospects *need* to achieve, because it gives an indication as to the smallest size the deal might become; knowing what a prospect *wants* to achieve makes the opportunity much bigger. Knowing what you want to achieve gives you the opportunity to realize it, as opposed to knowing what you need to achieve and just aiming for that. When we think of our most successful customers, we see that past successes can be a great predictor to help us understand what future customers can achieve. What are the patterns of the best deals? What deals closed the fastest, with the highest revenue? What specific people evaluated and bought (e.g., COO, CTO, CEO, VP, manager, etc.)? I have no doubt your service offers many benefits, but what is the most common problem being solved—the exact problem? This is not what your marketing team says your product does, or how we pitch the product, but the exact way the customer is using it and why that offers them value. If you look at the five best deals, two or three probably have very similar customer-use cases. Patterns are there to be found. For example, most successful customers will be using your service to solve a specific problem; similar people in each business will evaluate; and there will be very similar sales processes too. Assess the top five deals that were done over the last twelve months and see what the data tells you.

Prospecting ... Works?

To maximize success for your prospects and yourself, being brilliant at articulating the value your best customers get and taking prospects through the best sales cycle will benefit all involved. This specificity will also form the basis for messaging that resonates with prospects.

Give Yourself a Head Start

Most of the time, people compare only two or three solutions before they buy. This means you don't have to be the best sales-person in the world to win the business; you just need to be better than a few other salespeople you directly compete with. Most sales professionals rely on their experience, but elite sales professionals include the habit of preparation. It's like giving yourself a head start in a hundred-meter race. The amount of preparation can vary, as can the effectiveness of the prepara-tion. You could do a small amount of preparation, identifying the best possible outcome, and get a 1.9 meter head start; you could apply all six hidden habits and gain an 11.9 meter head start; or you could ignore preparation altogether and start 4.5 meters behind the competition! It will still be a close race, but preparing tilts the odds of winning more often in your favor. Usain Bolt won the Olympic gold medal for the hundred-meter race in 2008, 2012, and 2016, finishing approximately 2 meters, 1.2 meters, and 90 centimeters ahead of second place, respectively. Prospecting gets you into the race, and applying the hidden habits of preparation determines your head start. People will remember your big wins for years to come, but the deals that *almost* happened are forgotten immediately. When searching for new customers, knowing what you want to achieve, determining the possible outcomes, and applying professional preparation gives you a fair advantage, transforming you into Usain Bolt.

The big problem for people—ranging from solopreneurs to seasoned sales professionals—is that most believe searching for new customers works, but a lot of them think searching for new customers doesn't work for *them*! Some believe they should dedicate time to prospecting so they can find new customers, but others think it's not an efficient use of time. There is always something more "important" or "urgent" to do. For most, prospecting is done when the pipeline starts to dry up, which leads to sales coming in waves, with periods of success and periods of despair.

Most sales professionals create an annual plan to generate opportunities to exceed their sales targets, but they forget about it after a couple of months. The plan to generate a consistent pipeline of opportunities becomes a distant memory. The planned prospecting campaigns don't happen, and the intention to use personalized messages to connect with potential customers falls by the wayside. Sometimes people send generic messaging to the typical personas they sell to, but other times nothing gets sent. Prospecting out of necessity causes sales professionals to increase the volume of generic messages sent to possible customers. Despite more people being contacted, the general nature of the messaging means results rarely turn out as hoped. Because your research is condensed into a smaller period of time, it becomes more difficult to convey that you know what prospects are looking to achieve, or to work big-bet accounts. Prospecting campaigns become less effective as preparation becomes less specific.

A knock-on effect of not prospecting effectively is that you have fewer initial conversations with potential customers. Just as an athlete needs to play competitively to keep their skills sharp, you need to have regular qualification calls to maintain your ability to qualify opportunities you can close. The impact of not having regular initial calls with enough potential customers is that you are more likely to get "happy ears" and move some people into a sales cycle when they are just not ready. Needless to say, someone who is not well qualified will take your time—but most likely not your product.

Prospecting fails when you lack a clear understanding of what you are trying to achieve and ignore the positive impact it will have on your pipeline, career, and earnings. If you don't know the best possible outcome from your prospecting activities, then you will never reach it. Without a consistent pipeline of deals, you will suffer inconsistent sales, which will in turn affect your career. Choosing to ignore prospecting is akin to choosing to slow the momentum of your career. You may or may not believe in your ability to prospect and find new sales opportunities, but that doesn't matter. Rather than wondering if prospecting works for you, what's more important is *acting* like prospecting works and regularly connecting with potential customers to find opportunities to help them achieve more.

If you know your desired sales target for the year, do you know how many additional deals you need to prospect for and add to your pipeline to exceed your target? Calculating the pipeline gap for the rest of the year doesn't take long, but it's overlooked by so many.

No matter how busy you become, it's possible to carve out time to run an evergreen campaign to find new customers all year round. It's possible to strategically prospect big-bet accounts with relevant outcome-based content. It's also possible for your outreach to stakeholders to be personalized, meaningful, and crafted to trigger responses. You can hold yourself to higher standards for qualification calls and make more of those conversations contribute to your sales results. Making the effort to understand what potential customers want to achieve and incorporating the search for new customers into your routine will set you up for reaching or even exceeding your sales goals. This will give you the chance to work on better deals, grow your professional network, and increase your earnings because you bring more value to more people. Being disciplined and mastering the art of finding new customers will open the door to more career opportunities.

Now let's apply the achievement question to the three most common prospecting scenarios that most people encounter when looking for new customers. These are reaching out to people you don't know via cold outreach, running qualification calls, and running prospecting campaigns. Let's see what happens when we apply our thinking framework of the first hidden habit: *What are you looking to achieve?*

The Elite Salesperson Mindset

Prior to prospecting, sales, and promotion activities, elite salespeople always consider what the other person, themselves, and influential stakeholders are looking to achieve.

They quickly ask themselves the following questions: What is the best possible outcome? What are the broad possible outcomes? What are the career progression opportunities for everyone involved? Elite salespeoples' heightened awareness makes successful outcomes more likely. When they are not sure, they use curiosity to quickly seek clarification.

The three prospecting, sales, and career progression scenarios are purposefully designed as repetitious to help make it second nature for you to consider what the other person, you, and influential stakeholders are looking to achieve. They remind you to quickly think about the best possible outcome, broad possible outcomes, and career progression opportunities for your prospecting, sales, and career promotion activities.

Messages Worthy of Interruption

Cold outreach means interrupting someone's day, so how can we make it useful for our prospective customers? How can we put content in context so that it becomes relevant to the people we target? When was the last time you crafted a message and sent it to someone you had no prior relationship with?

Think about the next cold message you will send someone. What are you looking to achieve? Do you want to pique interest? Secure a meeting? Qualify a potential customer's timeline, fit, or decision-making authority? Achievement could be getting to speak with a prospect, obtaining dates on future renewals, or finding out they are just not interested.

What are your prospects looking to achieve from cold outreach?

- What's the best possible outcome of cold outreach for your prospect?

- What are the broad possible outcomes of this for your prospect?

- What's the career progression opportunity of cold outreach for them?

What are you looking to achieve with cold outreach for yourself?

- What's the best possible outcome of cold outreach for you?

- What are the broad possible outcomes for you?

- What's the career progression opportunity of cold outreach for you?

What are influential stakeholders looking to achieve from your cold outreach?

- What are stakeholders with influence over prospects looking to achieve?

- Who are the influential stakeholders that could open the door to the prospect (e.g., champion, end user, influencer, investor, economic buyer)?

- What's the best possible outcome of cold outreach for influential stakeholders?

- What are the broad possible outcomes of cold outreach for them?

Disqualified

Do you want to qualify the opportunity; understand the timeline, the budget, or the decision-making process; or determine who else needs to get involved? Clarifying the best possible outcome prepares you to be that much braver with your questions because they are more intentional and outcome-oriented. Sometimes aiming to disqualify prospects can have a greater impact on helping you find those prospects who really need your service.

**What are prospects looking to
achieve from the qualification call?**

- What's the best possible outcome for them?

- What are the broad possible outcomes and what is the potential career progression for them?

What are you looking to achieve from the qualification call?

- Consider the best and the broad possible outcomes. Sometimes it helps to write them down.

**What are the stakeholders with influence over the
prospect on the qualification call looking to achieve?**

- Are you aware of any stakeholders who have influence over your prospect (e.g., end user, influencer, investor, economic buyer)?

- From the stakeholders' perspective, what's the best possible outcome for them?

Be Deliberate

Successful prospecting campaigns fast-track you to overachieve. What other goals or objectives will benefit when you generate a consistent flow of qualified opportunities into the sales pipeline? Aligning prospecting with your big-picture goals will help you develop the right outcome-based focus for the campaign.

Should you home in on prospects and existing customers who want to evaluate your services, or should you focus on building a database of prospect renewal dates to target in the future? Does your product require partners to implement it, and would those partners want to participate in the prospecting campaign so they get the first opportunity to sell to the prospective customers with you?

As for your own goals, will you get to speak to more potential customers? Do you have the time or interest to speak with nonqualified prospects? If so, might you get better at articulating the value of your service? To add a strategic level to your preparation, it's important to anticipate potential challenges and how to overcome them.

What impact will a successful prospecting campaign have on your year?

- What long-term goals and objectives is this aligned with?

- What happens if you don't do this?

- What excites you about this?

- What are the biggest obstacles between you and your best possible outcome, and what will you do to overcome them?

What are the prospects of your prospecting campaign looking to achieve?

- What's the best possible outcome for the targeted prospects?

- What are the broad possible outcomes and career progression opportunities for them?

**What are you looking to achieve
with your prospecting campaign?**

- Consider the best possible outcome, the broad possible outcomes, and the career progression opportunities of the prospecting campaign. This also serves as motivation to help you prospect when nobody's looking.

**Are there influential stakeholders for some prospects?
What are they looking to achieve?**

- What's the best possible outcome for the stakeholders with influence?

- What are the broad possible outcomes and career progression opportunities for them?

Achieve More by Helping Others Achieve More

We get so submerged in the world of sales, going from deal to deal, task to task, that we often overlook what we're trying to achieve. Obviously, we are trying to sell more, sell faster, sell better, and earn as much commission as possible. But as our day unfolds and we go from one sales activity to another, the repetition of selling (combined with experience) causes us to assume everything will happen as it should. Most sales professionals don't think about the best possible outcomes from their sales activities and how they could fuel their career progression. They give their attention to next steps or whichever customers shout loudest, and they forget about what they're trying to achieve for their key customers and themselves. The outcome is often that they never get around to strategic activities that result in bigger long-term payoffs.

The experience that has got you this far in your career is most likely causing you to lower your standard of sales execution. Experience masks bad sales behavior and habits and leads sales professionals to believe they don't need to prepare. Experience will get you through a sales meeting, a whole deal cycle, or even an entire year without needing to do much preparation, but it causes you to miss opportunities. Mediocre sales meetings that result from a lack of preparation can cause you to waste more time and lose more deals than you should. Being unprepared to uncover what your customer is striving to achieve can cause you to run a complete sales cycle that just falls short of connecting the dots for the customer to buy. Some sales cycles run their course without the salesperson truly understanding what would have been required to get the deal signed. Sales can feel more like a race through all the steps of the cycle instead of a consultative process to understand what the customer is looking to achieve, quantify the value it will bring them, and agree together on how you will know you've achieved a successful outcome. In a sales cycle, you have a few opportunities to understand the key measures of success (more on this in chapter 9) and the outcomes the business is looking to achieve. This detail is glossed over too often! If you don't take even just a few minutes to prepare, it's more likely that you'll miss some key buying information from the customer, and even if you spend hours on the final pitch, you'll miss the key point to get the deal over the line.

How is the execution of your annual sales plan going? Or have you forgotten about it? If you don't create and iterate an annual sales plan, then you don't know your best possible outcomes, the broad possible outcomes, and what is at stake for your career progression. Experience will get you through the year and get you a respectable outcome, but without a plan, you will likely underachieve and have much less control over what you'll be doing next year. You'll more likely fill your calendar with urgent work rather than strategic sales activities that move the needle of performance. The pain of being forever busy in sales and getting average results is something I don't wish for anyone. Lacking a plan will also make your prospecting lead flow unpredictable and cause your career to falter.

If you know exactly what you want to achieve in a sales meeting, you are much more likely to achieve it. Experience will get you through the meeting, but preparation will get you the best possible outcome. Clarity also gives you a sense of purpose that prospects and customers respond positively to. You can accelerate success further by gaining clarity on your prospects' ideal outcomes. If you focus on high-value outcomes, you bring more passion and positivity to meetings, and you offer more value to your customers. When you achieve your objectives in sales meetings and customers exceed theirs, meetings are energizing and get everyone excited for the next one.

Similarly, when you look at the sales cycle, the clearer you are on the best and broad possible outcomes for your customer at key moments in the cycle, the more monetary value there is to capture. This is because the more transformational the project, the more business value you can provide. Often, when sales professionals meet existing accounts, they think relatively small. Typically, an upsell or cross-sell is the height of the ambition. But this perspective limits the opportunities sales professionals find. Add-on or upsell business offers less value to the customer than a transformational project. Customers tend to run the sales cycle a little more and look at other point solutions too, reducing the revenue potential of the deal. The outcomes of bigger deals are that they become larger sales and your sales cycles become more focused and progress faster. Faster deal cycles offer increased capacity to work even more deals. In contrast, a lack of preparation and clarity on your customers' outcomes can result in slow sales cycles or, even worse, elongated sales cycles that require extra resources to close. Holding yourself to this higher standard of preparatory thinking will help you close more deals faster and at a higher monetary value, and mastering your sales cycles in this way consistently breeds confidence, creating a virtuous circle that brings even more success.

Clarifying the best and broad possible outcomes for your annual sales plan can be the difference between a plan that is forgotten about versus an achievement engine that helps you drive a consistent flow of leads, run more successful sales cycles, and obtain exceptional sales results that will open doors for future career opportunities. You can have a plan that outlines what is needed to exceed your sales target, including a schedule for prospecting on a regular basis to ensure you have a steady flow of opportunities and for removing less important "urgent" work. With more deals to work, you can constantly work on improving preparation, which will improve the quality of outcomes, helping you achieve more. Executing an annual plan with repeatable processes to exceed your annual sales target builds momentum that grows as each sales milestone is reached.

Being aware of the range of best possible outcomes and having a plan to work toward them gives peace of mind that you are more likely to be satisfied with your effort and outcomes. The real payoff of knowing what you and your customers want to achieve in sales meetings and sales cycles is that they are more valuable and productive for both parties. Complicated sales cycles, with more people, variables, and deal dependencies, are more likely to close when you are working toward specific outcomes. Transformational projects that require more effort from both sides are more likely to be successful. The obvious payoff of commission from such deals is great, but it's also worth considering that these customers have a higher chance of becoming references and case studies too! The added benefit is that your career progression is more successful because you've created and executed a sales plan. Your mindset switches from expecting less and being delighted when something better happens to expecting the best possible outcome and being satisfied when it happens.

Let's explore three sales activities—the sales meeting, the sales cycle, and your annual sales plan—and apply the thinking framework for achievement to them. Some aspects of certain sales require multiple stakeholders, so make sure to consider a wide range of stakeholders when you apply this question.

Run Great Meetings

Bringing purpose to your sales meetings makes them more productive for everyone. This will also help you form more meaningful agendas for all involved. What type of sales meeting are you preparing for: qualification, discovery, demo, commercial presentation, quarterly review, or something else? Taking the time to consider the best outcome for meeting attendees means your meeting is much more likely to have a successful outcome.

What is your prospect looking to achieve in the sales meeting?

- Best possible outcome? Broad possible outcomes?

- Career progression?

What are you looking to achieve in the sales meeting?

- Again, consider your best possible outcome, the broad possible outcomes, and if career progression opportunities exist.

Are any influential stakeholders *not* in the meeting?

- What do they want your prospect to achieve?

- What is their potential gain?

Big Moments

Some sales cycles last a single meeting, most range between a few weeks or months, and some can be over a year! Think about a piece of business that will make a big impact on your year when you close it. What critical parts of your sales cycle are required to get the deal done? Each stakeholder has a different view on the deal, so consider as many perspectives as possible. Could what some stakeholders in the background are looking to achieve make them unexpected allies?

What is your prospect looking to achieve during the sales cycle?

- What's the best possible outcome of the sales cycle for your prospect?

- What are the broad possible outcomes for them?

- What's the career progression opportunity of the sales cycle for your prospect?

What are you looking to achieve in the sales cycle?

- What's the best possible outcome of the sales cycle for you?

- What are the broad possible outcomes for you?

- What's the career progression opportunity of the sales cycle for you?

What are influential stakeholders of the prospect in the sales cycle looking to achieve?

- Who are the influential stakeholders required to gain a positive outcome (e.g., users, influencers, investors, economic buyers)?

- What's the best possible outcome of the sales cycle for them?

- What are the broad possible outcomes for them?

More Important than Sales

The ability to formulate and execute an annual sales attainment plan is often called out by leadership as more important than the outcome of the plan itself. If a plan is working, it can be continued; if not, it can be changed. If no strategic plan exists, it's a lot more challenging to improve. Can you use your annual sales plan to show that you can create a strategic plan and execute it?

Your sales attainment plan is the bridge between your sales goals and sales execution. Will you build strategic relationships with prospects for high-value business or go in the opposite direction and focus on lower-value, higher-volume sales? A clear path to exceed your sales target will reduce stress, worry, and anxiety. How can you improve on last year? Prioritize high-value tasks? Create more innovative approaches? Do consistent prospecting? We can always improve, and reflecting on how to improve on last year is a great starting point.

What are the prospects you are targeting for your sales attainment plan typically looking to achieve?

- What are their best and broad possible outcomes?

- Can your solution help prospects advance their career?

**What impact will a successful sales
attainment plan have on your year?**

- What are your goals?

- What happens if you don't have a sales attainment plan?

- What excites you about the coming year?

- What are you looking to achieve with your annual sales plan?

- What are the best possible outcome, broad possible outcomes, and career progression opportunities?

- What are the biggest obstacles between you and your best possible outcomes, and what will you do to overcome them?

**What are influential stakeholders of prospects
you are targeting for your annual sales plan typically
looking to achieve?**

- What are the best and broad possible outcomes for influential stakeholders?

- Does your solution help influential stakeholders progress their interests?

Preparation Accelerates Careers

There are very few things that warrant fear from sales professionals. However, not knowing how you want your career to progress, and procrastinating on taking measures to progress it, should warrant a healthy fear, since this can hold you back for years! Sales professionals who lack a clear promotion path half commit to different roles and opportunities throughout the year, with the net result of getting stuck in their current position a couple of years too long. If you spend too much time in one position, you become less attractive to the job market, limit your future income, and risk getting stuck in a rut. This causes muted enthusiasm that can be mistaken for negativity, which causes all sorts of problems, from making it more difficult to run a successful campaign to gain a promotion to passing your final interview. Sometimes staying too long in a position can signal that you are too set in your ways, and it can sometimes mean you're perceived as un-coachable. This is one of the worst traits for sales professionals, and if a hiring leader senses this, they will drop you like a hot potato.

Knowing the next career step you want to achieve, being brave enough to share it with the world, and talking to the right people in advance offers a much better chance of the promotion becoming a reality. Not having an outcome to work toward makes it nearly impossible to conduct meaningful networking with hiring leaders and difficult to show passion in interviews. Sales professionals who lack commitment to their next role generally lose out in the interview process to those who fully commit early. In addition, if you're trying to pull together a campaign to gain a promotion, it's a challenge to avoid procrastination if you don't have an outcome in mind.

Having others' best outcomes in mind is also important for your career progression. A lot of teams and hiring leaders have problems, and those problems create opportunities for you. Take the time to determine what their problems are and how you will solve them when you are successfully promoted into the new role. Making the desired solutions to hiring leaders' problems the backbone of your interview strategy and campaign to gain promotion is a great way to get to the front of the line of talented competition going for the same role.

Knowing your desired outcomes with regards to prospecting and selling is the cornerstone of career progression.

The better you get at executing sales cycles oriented toward high-value outcomes, the more deals you'll close, the more money you'll earn, and the faster you'll get promoted. Closing large deals is the difference between a good career and a career that goes interstellar. Getting promoted not only puts more dollars in your pocket but also creates an aura of success around your personal brand. Career momentum is a force to be reckoned with.

Let's examine three career-path activities and use the thinking framework for achievement in career promotion. The three activities are networking with hiring leaders, doing interviews, and running a campaign to gain promotion.

Discovery Networking

You want the hiring leader to decide they want to hire you before the interview even takes place. Networking gives you the opportunity to make yourself the prime candidate for the role—you can make yourself the choice the hiring leader wants to make. What is the outcome the hiring leader is working toward? Where are they looking to progress their career to? Can you use networking sessions to build relationships with hiring leaders? What value can you offer them? For instance, can your conversation become a mini discovery session to uncover what else they need for their team? Can you use these networking meetings to build an interview pitch around the current pain points of the team? Can you discover the existing problems the leader is trying to deal with and transform them into an advocate for you in the interview process? Also, think about the wider decision-making team for your next role.

**What are hiring leaders looking
to achieve when networking?**

- What are the best and the broad possible outcomes of networking for leaders?

**What are you looking to achieve when
networking with leaders who are hiring?**

- What is the best possible outcome (e.g., they agree to sponsor you into the position)?

- What are the broad possible outcomes (e.g., they agree to
  join your interview panel, or they recommend other key
  people to network with)?

**What are you looking to achieve when networking with
stakeholders who can influence leaders who are hiring?**

- Who are the influential stakeholders whose recommendations will increase the likelihood of you getting an interview
  or the job? (e.g., second-, third-, or even fourth-line leaders and those who work closely with sales leadership, such
  as partners, sales strategists, business development, and
  customers)?

- What are the best and broad possible outcomes of networking with these stakeholders?

Where To?

If you know where you want to go, you have a chance of getting
there. If you know *why* you want to go, you have a chance of
doing the work once the initial burst of motivation wears off. If
you are going for an interview, you want to get a job offer with

the highest compensation possible. You want the hiring leader to be falling over themselves trying to hire you, and you want the internal leaders to be fighting with each other for you to join their team. So to get an exceptional offer, what are the various possible outcomes, and how will you make the best possible outcome more likely to happen for you?

What are interviewers looking to achieve in your interview?

- What are the best and the broad possible outcomes for the interviewers?

What are you looking to achieve in your interview?

- What are the best and broad possible outcomes of the interview for you?

- If you're successful in this interview, what do you envision the next position to be?

- Who are the influential stakeholders of interviewers who can sway a positive outcome (e.g., leadership, champion hiring leader, colleagues from the hiring team, influencers)?

- What's the best possible outcome of the interview for influential stakeholders?

- What are the broad possible outcomes of the interview for influential stakeholders?

The Multiplier Effect

Have you ever run a campaign to gain promotion? Most networking consists of "coffee and a chat" a few weeks ahead of an interview, tending to feel forced and awkward. If you run a promotion campaign, could you aim for getting promoted at the first time of asking, or convincing the hiring leader before the interview that you're a great fit for the role? Can you make connections with key people for future positions in your career too? Can you determine your long-term career goals and how to articulate them with passion? Can you build your brand with leadership and achieve more certainty of gaining promotion? As a result of hiring you, could the hiring leader progress their own career faster? Can the hiring leader's team perform at a higher level with you in it? These actions culminate in you bringing more value, which means better compensation.

**What impact will a successful
promotion campaign have on your year?**

- What long-term goals and objectives is this aligned with?

- What happens if you don't do this?

- What excites you about this?

- What are the biggest obstacles between you and your best possible outcome, and what will you do to overcome them?

**What are the leaders you are targeting
to promote you looking to achieve?**

- What's the best possible outcome of your promotion campaign for leaders who are hiring?

- What are the broad possible outcomes of your promotion campaign for these leaders?

- What's the career progression opportunity for them?

**What are you looking to achieve with
your promotion campaign?**

- What's the best possible outcome of your promotion campaign for you?

- What are the broad possible outcomes?

- What's the career progression opportunity of the promotion campaign for you?

**What are influential stakeholders of leaders who can
influence your promotion campaign looking to achieve?**

- Who are the influential stakeholders whose support is required to gain a positive outcome (e.g., leadership, champion hiring leader, colleagues from the hiring team, influencers)?

- What's the best possible outcome of the promotion campaign for stakeholders?

- What are the broad possible outcomes of the promotion campaign for them?

- What's the career progression opportunity of the promotion campaign for them?

CHAPTER SUMMARY

- Elite sales professionals are clear on what they want to achieve from prospecting, selling, and promotion activities.

- Shift your mindset from what you need to what you want (i.e., the best possible outcome).

- Prospecting is interrupting someone's day, so make it valuable for them.

- You just need to outperform the two or three salespeople competing with you for the deal.

- Salespeople who don't fully commit to a specific next role get stuck in current positions longer.

Chapter Questions for Hidden Habit #1:
What Are You Looking to Achieve?

Strategic Preparation:

- What's the best possible outcome?
- What are the broad possible outcomes?
- What's the career progression opportunity?

4

What Is the Current Situation?

Paul M. Caffrey

Long and rewarding journeys are best taken together. To do so, you all have to agree on the place to start as well as the desired direction.

PHIL M. JONES

COMPETITION? RELATIONSHIP? Catalyst?

Seeing the current situation as it really is makes it easier to determine what's required to reach your desired outcome. But assessing the current situation is like looking at the league table, or standings, in sports: it lets you know where you rank, but it can also be misleading! In a soccer league, your rank is based on points accumulated from the results of your games: 3 points for a win, 1 point for a draw, and nada if you lose. At the end of the season, after all games have been played, fans tend to agree that teams finish where they deserve based on their performances. It's the same in sales: at the end of the year, when all the meetings have been done and sales cycles are completed, your earnings tend to reflect the value you brought to your customers.

However, at certain points in the season, the league table can be skewed due to good or bad runs of results. It's important to have the maturity to identify if it's your performance or external factors causing you to go on a good or bad run. In sports, you can play a series of bad teams and win many games in a row. Similarly, in sales you can hit a streak where customers just want to buy and you close deal after deal. The other side of this coin is that in sports you can lose a number of games in a row, and in sales you can lose a number of deals in a row too!

Maintaining an actual understanding of your current situation, and if it's what your performances merit, is very important. It offers you the chance to take the right action at the right time to win more. The more you win, the higher your rank in the table. It doesn't matter if you're prospecting, running a deal, or on the promotion hunt: awareness of the actual current situation gives you a starting point for meaningful action to reach the success you're trying to achieve. Elite sales professionals assess the current situation again and again and achieve longer-lasting success year after year.

You might be closing deal after deal, and all might be great with the world, or you might be in a real rut, losing deal after deal, unsure where the next one will come from. What's important is seeing things exactly as they are, not better or worse. If you are taking action based on the current situations that evolve as a deal is worked, then you can have the confidence that you'll finish higher up the table.

Having the maturity to understand when a bluebird megadeal has landed in your lap is important. Having the maturity to know when something in your industry means prospects are frantic to buy is important. Sometimes you're having a great time that has nothing to do with you, such as the real estate boom for agents during COVID-19. In contrast, it's also important to know when the tide is against you—when, for example, deals are stagnating, or the wider industry is having a tough time. Sometimes you're going to have a bad time that has nothing to do with you, such as selling office space or travel software in 2020. Most of the time in sales, you work hard and deserve what you get—maybe not always in the short term, but over the long term, elite behavior is rewarded. Whether times are great or couldn't get much worse, elite sales professionals see the current situation for what it really is day after day and take calculated, impactful action. The analysis of the audio of over one million sales calls by Gong.io showed that sales professionals who sought to understand the current situation early in terms of competition had 24 percent higher win rates. Knowing the competition early gives you the ability to address them in your sales presentations later in the deal cycle.

At its core, business is a relationship where both parties benefit. Elite sales professionals are always aware of the quality of their relationships with their prospects, and they are also aware of prospects' relationships with competitors. Relationships are critical to success, and they can be dramatically improved over a short period of time.

Elite sales professionals also always make sure they understand the prospect's current situation by clarifying: Why change? Why now? Why our company? Is the evaluation to replace an existing solution? Is it a specific business outcome the prospect is working toward? Is it a wider initiative? Regardless of whether the prospect initiated contact or you reached out to them, they believe you may be able to help them improve their situation. Elite sales professionals will establish the pain of the current situation for the prospect and extrapolate what happens if the prospect buys their service versus competitors', and highlight what happens to the prospect if the decision date is missed or what the prospect loses out on if they make no decision. Is there real urgency with this project? Will the business be negatively affected commercially or otherwise if they don't proceed by a certain date?

We are all conditioned to organize our sales evaluations with prospects by sales stage—Stage 1: Initial Call, Stage 2: Qualified Opportunity, Stage 3: Discovery, Stage 4: Demo, etc. Elite sales professionals use the six questions in this book to prepare for each stage to ensure the next meeting is successful, and they are prepared to transition the prospect to the next step in the sales cycle.

Time for some truths. Nobody is going to check if you have assessed the current situation or done your due diligence on the competition, or if you understand the relationships or know the catalyst for the sales evaluation. You will know if you have done the preparation. But here is the real shocker: most people think it's the best products at the best prices that people buy, but it's not. People buy the solutions with the higher perceived business value. We say "perceived" because a better product with inferior sales professionals will lose to an inferior product with elite sales professionals because those professionals will connect the capabilities of their service with the business objectives of the customer, clearly showing how their service will directly turn the needle of performance for key business outcomes.

Sales is really just a value transfer game. You can choose to play the game and hope your natural ability to connect the value of your product to customers' needs on the spot is enough to beat your rival sales professional, or you can assess the current situation and, with preparation, give yourself a fair advantage to win the deal. Small actions add up over time, and just as a single penalty kick can win the game, a little preparation can make the difference in connecting your service to an outcome the customer is striving toward. Over the course of a year, fine margins add up to have a massive impact, moving you to the top of the league table.

Connect with People's
Current Situations and Lead the Way

When prospecting isn't working, the reason often cited is, "We aren't reaching the right people," but that is rarely the case. Nobody likes to hear it, but generally the message isn't speaking to where the prospect is today and where they want to go. Whether you're sending messages to people you've never spoken with or running a full-scale prospecting campaign, if you don't understand their current situation and their competitive landscape, and if you don't have an idea of how you can improve their business, why would they waste their time responding to you?

Low lead flow is stressful, both for the business and for your pocket. Business development gets anxious, and desperation makes prospecting even harder. Sales professionals' pipelines start to dry up, and negativity creeps in. The pipelines' quality drops, and it can become difficult to predict when normality will return. However, it is possible to change fortunes when prospecting hits a bumpy road. Knowing your prospects' current situation prevents you from getting into the precarious position of a small pipeline.

So where is the prospect today? Is there software that will tell you what technology they use, or intelligence on your customer relationship management (CRM) platform? Who are your main competitors? I'm guessing your prospects are using one of your rivals, or perhaps they don't have a solution at all. Do you understand the competitive landscape—the types of competitors in your ecosystem, their strategies, and how they compete with you? Do you have a relationship with the prospect? Do you routinely reach out to key contacts? When dialogues start, do you know the catalyst for the call in the first place?

For qualification calls, it's possible to determine if you are in a competitive situation and what happens to the prospect's business if they decide not to buy any solution at all. Is there an existing or previous relationship with your company that you can leverage? Prospects respond well to industry expertise and an understanding of their current position. Getting a response to a beautifully crafted outbound communication and those initial self-generated leads is exciting because they can become the foundation for continual lead flow. Clear messages that connect with where prospects are today will generate more leads, make it easier to qualify more opportunities, and bring your prospecting effectiveness to the next level.

Apply the current-situation question when you reach out to people you don't know via cold outreach, qualification calls, and prospecting campaigns. Let's see what happens when we understand the current situation.

Your Message Is the Bridge

Connecting with someone's current situation and showing yourself as the bridge to their desired state is the ultimate goal of cold outreach. When you are entering someone's world uninvited, connecting with their situation increases the chances of getting a response. Challenging yourself to empathize with them will reframe your outreach in a more meaningful way. How does your message speak to the prospect's current situation versus the countless others competing for their attention?

What is the current situation for prospects you're sending cold outreach?

- Have you had success with a prospect's competitor that you can share?

- Has your prospect had a relationship with you or your business from a previous role?

- What will be the catalyst to trigger a response from your prospect?

What is the current situation for cold outreach for you?

- Is your prospect using a competitor?

- What personal connection exists that could start a relationship (e.g., introduction via mutual connections on a professional social network; similar shared experiences or interests like university or sport)?

- What's your catalyst for reaching out to the prospect? Why now?

New Opportunities Deserve a Blank Canvas

Confirmation bias causes sales professionals to interpret new information as confirmation of their existing beliefs about the prospect and their business. Consider the information you have, but be open-minded in your preparation for a qualification call, and make sure to validate your thoughts on the call as much as possible. Sales professionals who take this approach do not gloss over obvious questions, and as a result they rarely miss an opportunity their confirmation bias tells them does not exist.

The earlier that sales professionals know the competition (if a relationship or loyalty already exists and what the driver is for change now), the more likely a successful sales outcome becomes.

What is the prospect's current situation for the qualification call?

- Who is your prospect's biggest competition? Have you worked with any of them?

- Who does the prospect know that might have a relationship with you?

- What do you think is the catalyst for the prospect to speak with you (e.g., did they share any info on their inbound request or on the response to outbound prospecting)?

What is your current situation for the qualification call?

- Is your prospect also evaluating your competitors?

- What is the existing relationship between you or your business and your prospect?

- What is the catalyst for the qualification call for you (e.g., inbound or outbound)?

You're Not on the List

Prospecting campaigns are most effective when you decide who you're *not* prospecting to. This is difficult, as we naturally feel that casting our net wider gives a better chance of finding new business. Some specific criteria, such as size, industry, and region, are probably already defined for you. Sometimes it's easier to replace certain solutions for prospects, as opposed to getting a prospect who does not use any comparable solution to use yours. Prioritizing prospects who have a relationship with you or your business is another lens to use. Catalysts to narrow the prospecting field can also include funding, new leadership, changes in head count, new regulation, and renewal dates for current solutions. This is not an exhaustive list, as every business will have specific fields unique to their business and industry too.

What led to your current situation to run a prospecting campaign, and how will it be better than your last one?

- Are your prospects typically using a competitor?

- What is the existing relationship between you and your prospects?

- Twelve months ago, what was your situation for your prospecting campaigns?

- What strategies for prospecting campaigns have you used before? What worked or did not work?

- What exactly needs to happen to bring the current situation toward the best possible outcome?

- What impact will this have on your situation next year?

What is the current situation for prospects you are targeting with the prospecting campaign?

- What signature customers do you work with that prospects may recognize as competitors?

- Who do your prospects know that might have a relationship with you?

- What's the typical catalyst for prospects to speak with you?

What's Really Going On?

Making assumptions early in the sales cycle tends to cause issues that can lead to delays, roadblocks, and even the dreaded "closed lost" outcome. When these situations arise, it means something critical was missed earlier in the sales process. There can be countless reasons why sales don't happen, but more often than not, it comes down to how you compete with the competition, the strength of relationships, and lacking a compelling event.

It's important to assess the current situation with a paranoid mindset and try not to overlook anything. The lack of competition can be a great warning sign. If the prospect is serious about the project, then why are they only talking to you? As surprising as it sounds, not all sales professionals confirm their competition with the prospect early in the sales process. Knowing your competition early dramatically increases your likelihood to win the business.

Establishing the competitive situation will give you more credibility in your prospect's eyes, which helps you build the relationship too. The stronger the relationship between you and your prospect, the more likely it is that you'll achieve a successful outcome. Sometimes the relationships between prospects and your competitors are overlooked. People assume that if the prospect is giving them a lot of time and attention, then everything is okay, and the paranoia of thinking about the competition is naively forgotten about. This is especially misleading, as the prospect could be giving the competition a lot of attention too.

Getting a lot of time from a prospect is a good indicator that there is business to be won, but your prospect talking to a competitor is a better indicator. The catalyst for the conversation is the ultimate indicator of whether or not there is business to be won. If the catalyst is a compelling event, which means the prospect needs to take action and will lose out financially if they don't, well, that's the kind of catalyst that brings the urgency required to get the deal done. If the catalyst is a compelling event twelve months away, or the prospect just wants to learn more about your product, it's much harder to get the deal closed.

So what happens if you know the current situation? Knowing the competition early means you can align with what the prospect is looking to achieve and point out key differences between achieving this with you versus your competitor. If your competitor is particularly strong in an area you are not, you can raise this with your prospect and confirm early whether or not this will make the difference in you winning the business. Then if that particular strength comes up again in the sales cycle later on, you can get past it and still have a chance to win the business.

Knowing the strength of your relationship with the prospect, as well as their relationship with the competitor, enables you to take corrective action if required. If you believe you require a stronger relationship, being aware of this will spark your mind to figure out how to achieve it. If a relationship with a competitor is a concern, you can address that directly and find out if you really have a fair chance to win their business.

Gaining clarity on the catalyst for the prospect to kick off an evaluation goes a long way toward forecasting if and when the deal is signed. Knowing about a compelling event for the prospect gives the urgency required for a timebound decision to be made. Knowing all these aspects of the current situation means you can prioritize the deals you spend time working on.

The Real Deal?

In preparation for sales meetings, the current situation framework gives you a starting position to determine and understand the competition, relationships, and catalysts. These can be validated in the meeting and may help form the basis for the next steps. Are you ahead or behind? Strong or weak in a certain area? Are you missing something? Is this a real sales meeting or are you just making up the numbers?

What is your prospect's current situation for the sales meeting?

- Who is your prospect's biggest competition? Have you worked with any of them?

- Who does your prospect know that might have a relationship with you?

- What do you think is the catalyst for your prospect to meet you?

What is the current situation of the sales meeting for you?

- Is your prospect using a competitor? Is your prospect evaluating your competitors?

- What is the existing relationship between you and your prospect?

- What connection exists that could bolster the relationship (e.g., mutual connections in a professional social network or a shared experience or interest)?

- What is the catalyst for the sales meeting?

What is the current situation of influential stakeholders of the prospect at the sales meeting?

- What is your current relationship with influencers on the decision? How can it improve?

- What outcome would be the catalyst for influencers on the decision to support changing the current situation?

Everyone Wants Something

We commit to a sales cycle with prospects with qualified needs, understanding their current situation, when business is to be won. Few consider the current situation of the sales cycle itself. Prospects are looking for someone, not necessarily you, to solve their problem. If they don't have a relationship with you or your business, they want to know who does and, more importantly, if you helped them. We want to know how our relationships compare to the competition and gain a fair advantage to win the business. Sales cycles call for prudent paranoia because the competition is actively persuading the prospect to do business with them instead of you.

What is the prospect's current situation entering the sales cycle?

- What mutual customers or competitors to the prospect do you work with that are worth sharing during the sales cycle?

- Which of your existing customers have a relationship with your prospect or their business that you can reference and recommend they speak with?

- What is your prospect's catalyst for committing to the sales cycle, and how will your solution solve their problem?

What is the current situation of the sales cycle for you?

- Who are you competing with for the business? What fear, uncertainty, and doubt (FUD) will your competitors express about your business? How do you win against the specific competitors you are up against?

- What will you do to build a strong relationship with your prospect during the sales cycle?

What is the current situation of influential stakeholders of the prospect entering the sales cycle?

- Are any influential stakeholders connected with your competition?

- How will you build a relationship with them throughout the sales cycle?

- What's the catalyst for influencers to support changing the current situation and advocating your solution?

Consistently Do the Basics to a High Standard

A great predictor of how successful a sales attainment plan will be is to review what happened in the last twelve months within the specific patch of prospects, the wider business, and the industry as a whole. Trends such as who prospects compete with to win business, the types of relationships prospects demand in order to work with someone, and what actually makes prospects take action are a great starting point for any plan.

Improving on last year's performance means being honest with yourself about what you actually did and holding yourself

accountable to do activities that will have an impact this year
(e.g., setting time and actually prospecting, or maintaining
standards throughout your sales cycles, such as being prepared
consistently).

**What is the current situation of your sales attainment
plan compared to last year, and how can it be enhanced?**

- What factors and decisions led to your current situation?

- In previous years, what worked and what didn't?

- What exactly needs to happen to bring the current situation
  toward the best possible outcome?

- What impact will this have on your situation next year?

What's Missing?

We all know people who have been unsuccessful in their
attempts to get promoted despite their perfect interview
pitches and excellent sales performance. They probably deserve
a promotion but missed a key ingredient in their promotion
campaign—honestly acknowledging their current situation.
Perhaps they failed to understand where leadership ranked
them versus other candidates because they didn't network
with the hiring leaders in advance. Or perhaps they struggle to explain why they want to leave their current position
because they haven't created a promotion campaign to get
them from where they are to where they want to go. Not only
are extra years in the same position demoralizing, but you
also collect repeated experience that you likely won't need
for future positions.

You can bet that your competition knows the gaps in their experience and expertise for their next role and that they're taking action to address them and telling every hiring leader they meet exactly what they are doing.

If you're moving from sales development to sales, you'll probably lack experience delivering sales presentations and negotiating commercials. Arrange to sit in on three or four sales presentations and one or two negotiations so you can share what you learn and how you plan to try to close deals in your interview.

If you're moving into people management for the first time, sitting in on interviews for new hires and understanding how to run the interview and score the candidate takes effort, but guess what? When the lack of hiring experience comes up in your interview, you can share what you learned from sitting in on interviews in preparation for the role.

Remember that sales is not just about numbers—it's also about relationships. Networking with hiring leaders may make you cringe, but it's super necessary to get ahead, as it's an opportunity to demonstrate the vital sales skill of networking itself. Typically, hiring leaders have some urgency when they interview. It could be to get someone to join, to onboard them for a few months with a lower ramped target while they are learning the business (e.g., they may hire someone and get them ready to sell for the start of the upcoming financial year). Finding this out in your networking conversations means you can speak to it in your interview.

There is no better feeling than entering an interview with the confidence of knowing you've networked with the interviewers, and they know exactly what they are getting with you. Even if the interview goes badly, you still have a chance of getting the job. If you have been previously unsuccessful going for promotion, that is an ideal starting point to share the second time around. You can demonstrate that you're adaptable and responsive to feedback by explaining why you were unsuccessful, what you learned from the feedback, and how you used it to fill gaps and progress to your current situation, in which you're now truly ready for promotion. Sometimes being unsuccessful is good because it gives you time to get even better.

More Important than the Interview

The reality is that most hiring leaders are looking for someone who can do the role, who they will get along with, and who will add to the team dynamic. It's difficult to get all of that across in a one-off interview, especially when the focus tends to be on experience and set questions to judge competence. Networking with the hiring leader is an opportunity to understand what they want, what you're missing, and what your competition's chances are (e.g., Do other candidates have a strong relationship with the hiring leader, or have they been invited to apply for the position?). These networking opportunities can be just as influential, and sometimes more so, as the interview itself on determining who gets the position.

What is the current situation for leaders who hire when they network?

- What competition do leaders networking for top talent face?

- When leaders network with you, do they network on an ongoing basis, or is there a specific catalyst?

What is your current situation networking with leaders?

- Is the leader networking with your competition?

- What is the existing relationship between you and the leader?

- What is your catalyst for networking with the leader? Did you contact them, or were you invited for a chat?

What is your current networking situation with stakeholders who have influence on the hiring leader?

- Are stakeholders who have influence with hiring leaders meeting other candidates?

- Can you build a relationship with a stakeholder to gain their recommendation of you?

- What action can you take to be the catalyst for the stakeholder of influence to recommend you to the hiring leader?

Why Are You Better?

Interviewers want you to make their job easier. They have the unenviable task of meeting the best version of candidates and having to somehow pick someone. They are then somewhat responsible for the success of the hire in the business, and let's face it: we have all heard about the horror-show hires and wondered how they got in the door!

Most people think the interview is to determine whether you can do the job, but being invited for an interview means that the interviewer likely already thinks you can do the job. The actual situation is whether you can do the job better than the other candidates. Elite sales professionals will focus on showing the competencies the interviewer is looking for and also look to differentiate themselves from the competition. Why should you be hired over other candidates? Do you explicitly share those reasons, examples, and stories to make it obvious for the interviewer?

The current situation is also the employer's needs for this role. Do you understand the landscape of the role you're looking to join? What prepared questions will you bring to the interview to show this? What relationships are you building that will help you get the role and perform in it?

What is the interviewer's current situation for the interview?

- Who is the interviewer's biggest competition? Why might you not take the job?

- Who do interviewers know that also have a relationship with you?

- What is the catalyst for your interview? Were you headhunted or did you apply?

What is the current situation of the interview for you?

- Who are your competitors, and what are three reasons you're a better hire?

- Is there an existing relationship between you and the hiring leader?

- What can you do to improve your relationship with the interviewer(s) before the interview?

What Else Can You Offer?

What are your chances of promotion, and how can you tilt the odds in your favor when you campaign for promotion? It starts with seeing your current situation for what it is. How do you compare to other candidates? What can you do to highlight your strengths and improve your weaknesses? Where does the interview panel and leadership rank you today versus the likely competitors for the role? If you're not at the top of the list, what can you do to change that?

Put yourself in the shoes of leadership and consider what challenges they have beyond requiring a new hire. Typically, everyone on a sales team can sell, but the team requires more than that. Prospecting, running events, and philanthropy; working with a large internal network; and having a desire to learn, share best practice, and challenge each other... the list goes on. The leader and team members will know what they are missing and will happily share that with you—because if you can tick one of those missing boxes, it helps the whole team.

Knowing how you complete the puzzle of the perfect sales team is half the battle. Next, you need the hiring leaders to find out. The biggest part of a great promotion campaign is finding influential people who will advocate for you with the hiring leaders. The higher the standing of the person advocating for you, the better, but don't let that put you off. If you can't get an influential leader on board, consider colleagues, customers, and even partners, if your business works with them.

What is the current hiring situation for leaders?

- What are their team's biggest challenges? What competition does their team face on a regular basis?

- Does their hiring leader work with anyone who knows you?

- What's the typical catalyst for candidates to network with hiring leaders? How can you get ahead of this?

What is the current situation of your campaign for promotion?

- Which candidates are your biggest competition? Why?

- What are your perceived gaps, and how can you show you are improving them?

- What can you do to network and build a relationship with leaders who are hiring?

- What are the three reasons you should be hired ahead of everyone else?

What is the current situation for stakeholders, such as senior leadership?

- Do senior leaders compete with each other for new hires?

- What is your current relationship with stakeholders who might influence the hiring leader's decision?

CHAPTER SUMMARY

- Understanding the current situation for what it really is allows you to take thoughtful, considered action.

- Connect with someone's current situation and show yourself as the bridge to their desired state.

- Business relationships can be dramatically improved over a short period of time.

- Nobody checks if you do the work before the work, but your performance will reflect it.

- Overlooking current situations can cause delays, roadblocks, and lost opportunities.

- Network with hiring leaders to understand what their current situation requires that isn't on the job specification.

Chapter Questions for Hidden Habit #2:
What Is the Current Situation?

Strategic Preparation:

- What's the competition?
- What relationships exist?
- What's the catalyst?

5

HIDDEN HABIT #3

What Is the Decision- Making Process?

Paul M. Caffrey

Before starting to dance, **learn the steps.**

PHIL M. JONES

HO? WHY? When?

This is it, Todd's big interview. He is determined to deliver an exceptional performance despite recently having a tonsillectomy. *Do I need to go to the emergency room?* he asks himself. *No, I'm okay; my throat's not bleeding. Time to start my promotion interview!*

The next hour will determine where he will work for the next year. Why do an interview when you're not 100 percent? When you have a genuine reason, why not reschedule? Because it isn't the interview that will determine if you get the role. The interview is only a single point of influence in the bigger decision-making process. Understanding all of the points of influence gives you the possibility of getting the promotion, even if the interview goes badly. You can still get the positive result you're working toward.

It's the same in sales: the demo is simply a single point of influence in the decision-making process, and it receives more attention than it deserves. It's important to zoom out and realize that the outcome the prospect is working toward isn't to receive a brilliant demo; it's to confirm that your product will improve their business. Once this is established, you can begin to persuade the decision makers that your service is a better option than going with the competition or remaining with the status quo.

Todd was on day five of his recovery from the tonsillectomy. He had excruciating pain while swallowing, ear canal irritation, and a constant headache. He could have requested to reschedule the final interview, but as a top performer, having run a great eight-month promotion campaign that went above and beyond, he made the decision to proceed. Everyone believed the pressure was on to deliver, but Todd knew it wasn't so important.

The interview went well, but Todd was a little flat, with his energy decreasing and discomfort on the rise as the painkillers started to wear off. This had all the hallmarks of becoming a hard-luck story... but it didn't! So often people think the interview is the only thing that matters to get the job. But if you understand the decision-making process, like Todd did, you can meet the influential people in advance, understand what's important for their decision, and share what they will get by choosing you. This mitigates the risk of a bad interview or a poor demo due to something beyond your control. By sharing your pitch in advance, you ensure the decision makers don't miss anything important in the interview. The interview serves as a reminder of *why* they should hire you, as opposed to them trying to figure out *if* they should hire you.

When it came to getting promoted, Todd had addressed a few factors in advance. He knew which hiring leaders were tasked with making the final decision, which people would give their opinions, and the selection criteria important to each person of influence. He ensured that his networking conversations with hiring leaders and influencers provided three clear reasons why he should be promoted over the competition. These were repeated throughout the interview, and Todd took the time to make them clear and memorable.

Todd also knew that the final decision hinged on two conversations, the first one being directly after his interview, when he would be scored. The second critical conversation would involve the hiring leaders comparing him to the other candidates who had passed the interview. Todd knew that senior leadership who were not in the interview would be discussing and ranking all candidates and would have major input in who to hire. He had taken time months in advance to meet the senior leadership team involved in this ultimate meeting. When the hiring team convened to make their decision, the key decision makers were all in agreement about Todd's abilities, and each one knew why they should hire Todd ahead of the others.

If Todd had not done the work before the work, he would not have gotten the promotion. One of the hiring leaders told him he hadn't given the best interview, but the team had learned enough about him throughout the process to be certain he was the best choice.

Important decisions that affect you are made all the time without you being there. It can be a decision about your promotion, or it can be prospects deciding whether to buy your service. These moments have a huge impact on your success as a sales professional, but most of the time you won't be in the room when the decisions are made. Often the conversations are shorter than you would imagine, and just a few critical pieces of information are discussed. To ensure that more of these decisions go your way, take the time to think about the who, why, and when of the decision-making process to create a fair advantage for yourself.

When Human Intelligence Trumps A.I.

A great place to start is to visualize the decision-making process your prospects use. Who tends to make the decision to purchase, when do they tend to do so, and which people in what positions influence the decision? Why would they choose you over your competition? Often your business will have standard personas they sell to and marketing-approved content to share. As a sales professional, you must do what artificial intelligence (A.I.) struggles with, which is getting the right content in front of the prospect within the right context at the right time. A.I. just doesn't have the data to do this for us today. The demand for 40 percent year-on-year hyper-growth driven by tech companies creates a culture of prospecting quantity over quality that can spill over into other industries and make it difficult to find time to consider how prospects make decisions. However, the truth is, you can save time by thinking about your prospect's decision-making process before you prospect.

When consideration is put into prospecting in terms of who makes the decision, why they make it, and when they make it, you are more likely to get the right content in front of the right prospect in the right context. This makes prospects more likely to invite you to meet, and it also reduces the duplication of effort later in the sales cycle. For instance, certain members of the C-suite who may have a deciding vote on your deal might request demos you already delivered. Clarifying the roles the C-suite will play in the evaluation often removes duplication of work throughout the evaluation.

When prospecting and getting a response, it's helpful to know that the final steps to getting a deal signed may require the chief financial officer's blessing. In the discovery session, you can offer to share the return on investment (ROI) for the prospect to validate. Surprise, surprise: the CFO will likely be asked to validate the ROI. This project is now on the CFO's radar early, with the business value and ROI validated.

Confirming the decision-making process in qualification calls means you'll include the right people in the sales cycle at the right time and have a better-qualified opportunity to work.

Asking yourself questions about the decision-making process throughout prospecting campaigns saves time, lowers the chance that you'll waste effort, and gets you as close as can be to the room where decisions are made.

Let's get back to our three prospecting scenarios and think about your prospects' decision-making processes.

Sometimes Prospects Really Want to Speak to Someone in Your Business—but Who?

Prospects respond to cold outreach when they are excited to speak to someone who can solve a problem. Sometimes it's you they are excited to speak with, and other times it's experts within your business. It's worth considering the best people to target. Be mindful that in a smaller business, the CEO might be involved, but a larger business might have a director responsible for buying the solution. Working your network of contacts and customers might offer another way into these prospects. Why do prospects get super excited to work with your business, and what are the lasting impacts and outcomes that successful customers enjoy? What small spark can your cold outreach ignite?

What is the decision-making process of prospects who receive cold outreach?

- Who in your business will your prospect be most excited to speak with (e.g., leadership, sales expert, technical team, other customers, etc.), and why?

- When will you let the prospect know that you can set up a conversation (if you can)?

What is the decision-making process for cold outreach for you?

- What people within the business are you targeting for cold outreach, and why?

- When will cold outreach have the best chance of getting a response?

- What medium will you use?

Use the Balance of Power to Establish the Exact Decision-Making Process

The qualification call is one of the few times sales professionals hold the balance of power, as prospects typically want information, a demo, or a trial of your services. Sales professionals get to decide how easy or challenging to make this for the prospect. How much information do you want to know about the prospect's decision-making process before committing your time and resources to them? The information you need could be who has direct input on the decision, who influences the decision, who makes the final decision, and who you need to get excited about the solution. It's also important to know when and how decisions are made.

Understanding the prospect's decision-making process is arguably the most important part of the qualification call because without a decision, nothing happens. Elite sales professionals spend a little extra time working through the possible scenarios. Sometimes the prospect will struggle to articulate how their company makes decisions and buys; pivot to asking them to share the story of how they bought similar solutions before. This will give clues as to how the prospect will buy from you.

What is the prospect's decision-making process?

- Who else in your business might the prospect want to speak with before making a decision (e.g., a call with senior leadership, a reference call, a call with customer support), and why?

- When will the conversation happen?

What is your decision-making process for the qualification call?

- What information do you want from the prospect before offering them an evaluation?

- Who is the ultimate decision maker, what's their decision criteria, and when will they make a decision?

- When will the prospect and their stakeholders get together to make the final decision?

- What's the compelling event?

- What happens if they don't make a decision? What are the consequences for the business?

What is the decision-making process of influential stakeholders?

- Who will have direct input on the decision, and who else will be included in the evaluation?

- Who will have indirect influence on the decision?

- Why will decision influencers choose a vendor? What's their decision criteria?

How Would a CEO Craft
Your Prospecting Campaign?

If you are working for a Fortune 500 company, it's likely you will have a tiny number of named accounts to prospect. If you're an entrepreneur or working in a start-up/scale-up, you'll have a wider net. Regardless of your exact situation, you will have to understand what resources you have and what the decision-making process is to make them available, and you'll also need to put your prospect first to get a response.

From a strategic perspective, some considerations for your prospecting campaign might be: Do you decide your own campaigns? Who else helps you? Who in the business decides what you should prospect for? Is the decision to prospect part of a strategic prospecting plan of your business, or is it your initiative to sell more? Why would sales development and product specialists decide to help (or not help) your prospecting efforts? Why does leadership get involved in prospecting projects? What alternative approaches to prospecting can leadership bring? When is the most effective time for you to decide to run prospecting campaigns? When should product experts and sales development get involved? When would leadership typically decide to offer extra support?

What is the decision-making process to determine the resources your prospecting campaign gets?

- What resources are required for the prospecting campaign? What support is needed?

- Who makes the decision to give you resources or support for the campaign?

- What impact will the decision have for them?

- What criteria will the decision makers use to decide whether to support you?

**What are prospects' decision-making
processes to respond to prospecting campaigns?**

- Why do prospects typically decide to accept your invitation for a meeting?

- Who else in your business do prospects want to speak with before making a decision?

- When a client has a problem, how much research do they do before deciding to speak to a salesperson?

**What is your decision-making process
to offer an evaluation to prospects who respond
to the prospecting campaign?**

- What does a typical sales evaluation comprise (e.g., discovery session, demo, proof of concept, commercial session, implementation overview, etc.)?

- Who is the ultimate decision maker (i.e., the typical persona)?

- What's the prospect's typical decision criteria?

- When do typical decisions get made?

- What are typical compelling events?

- What happens if prospects do nothing?

What is the decision-making process for influential stake-holders of prospects targeted by the prospecting campaign?

- Who else typically has input on the decisions?

- Why will decision influencers choose a particular vendor?

- What's their typical decision criteria?

- When do prospects and their stakeholders get together to make final decisions?

Don't Leave the Decision-Making Process to Chance

Generally, sales professionals can run a near-perfect sales cycle but do not get to speak with every stakeholder who has input on the decision. The invisible stakeholders' power can range from general influence to being the person who makes the ultimate decision. A middle manager may need to take a proposal to an executive for sign-off, an executive may need to take a proposal to the CEO/CFO for sign-off, the proposal may need to be taken to the board for approval, or perhaps investors behind the business need to sanction the spend before the contract gets signed. As much as we can challenge ourselves to speak to all of these stakeholders, sometimes it just isn't possible.

There is nothing worse than the sense of limbo when your proposal is being taken in-house for approval. If you are lucky, you may know that the prospect is having an internal meeting to discuss it, or when it's going to the board for sign-off. However, the dread sets in as you realize that the champion now has to sell this internally. Sometimes the solutions are complex, and the value is difficult to articulate. Sometimes there is a bias for the status quo. Sometimes champions are so close to a project that they don't properly explain the impact of not solving the problem. Sometimes they've bought into the project so much that they may have turned down a return-on-investment (ROI) justification. You are then relying on their ability to share the ROI verbally. During this time, you wonder what steps are happening in these meetings to decide if your weeks or months of work will result in a deal, further negotiation, or even worse—no decision at this time. (For the record, no decision is worse than a no, because if it's the latter, at least you know where you stand and can move on.)

You can't eliminate the risk of these invisible stakeholders not seeing the value, but you can do your utmost to mitigate it. The earlier you know exactly who is involved in the decision-making process, why they are making their decision, and when the decision is made, the better equipped you are to influence it. Sometimes the prospecting or very early qualification stage presents a relatively nonthreatening opportunity to clarify the final steps to closing a deal, as they are barely visible on the horizon for the customer. The final meeting of the stakeholders to discuss your project is particularly important.

Imagine how good it would feel to know the exact final decision-making steps your prospect is taking to rubber-stamp your deal and proceed. Imagine how much more at ease you would be knowing that the champion has a great version of the presentation with clear messaging, value proposition, and the cost of making no decision in terms that people will understand. It would feel even better if you managed to get fifteen-minute one-on-one conversations with some of the invisible stakeholders. It's important not to share so much information with your champions, stakeholders, and invisible stakeholders—whether it's the CEO, the CFO, or the board—that they are overwhelmed, but make sure they aren't given too little information either. It would be so great to know that your champion could present a single slide that shows the value and return on the project, and the required value your company delivers above the competition, which in turn minimizes the champion's need to figure out how to "sell" the project internally.

When the final decision-making process is completed and you become vendor of choice, that is when the real fun can begin. Some deals can have up to three negotiations: the champion will expect to bring a discount to the business, the CEO may push back for a discount as well, and then in the final stages the CFO will probably push for better terms too. Sometimes instead of giving a discount, it's worth exploring payment terms (e.g., semiannual instead of annual, preferred start dates, or invoicing net forty-five days instead of net thirty days for payment). Sometimes structuring the terms of the contract is better for the customer, as it's better for their accounting, and better for you, as you maintain more revenue. It's important to understand this in advance to keep your commercials competitive. Never give too much away early in a deal—you never know when it will be needed. Never discount much further than the original discount offered to the champion, either, because that damages your relationship and credibility with the person who sponsored you into the business. Another word of warning: No matter their title or seniority, don't assume the person knows how to buy or knows how their business will buy. Clarify how previous solutions were bought, and look for gaps in your buyer's decision-making process this time around.

It's a great feeling to get the call from your champion asking, "Can you send me an order form? I'm ready to proceed." Ultimately, knowing the exact last steps required to get a deal closed will increase your win percentage and forecasting accuracy. Both are great things for earning today and into the future.

This is where the rubber meets the road, as we delve into the nuances of the decision-making process for some sales situations we encounter regularly: sales meetings, sales cycles, and annual sales plans. Let's dig into the who, why, and when of the decision-making process for these three activities.

Understand Their Decision-Making Process before Progressing the Opportunity

When there is a sales meeting, do you know who is actually making the decision? The reality of decision making is there are no right or wrong answers for prospects, and in a sales meeting, people make decisions quickly. As a sales professional, you are working toward securing the next step at the end of the meeting. Having a strong idea on who, why, and when decisions will be made during the sales meeting will make you more effective in the meeting. The prospect may not be ready to progress to the next stage, but understanding the decision-making process means that you can confidently decide what happens next (e.g., progress the deal, finish working with the prospect, or continue to nurture them until they are ready to evaluate). Make sure all outcomes are considered. You can have confidence in your actions and be proud you did the right move by your business, even if the move was to walk away from the opportunity.

What is the prospect's decision-making process for the sales meeting?

- Who else in your business might the prospect want included in the sales meeting to make a decision (e.g., a call with senior leadership, a reference call, a call with customer support, etc.)?

- Why will the prospect want to speak with someone before making a decision?

- When will you set up specialist conversations (e.g., a security discussion) after the meeting?

What is your decision-making process for the sales meeting?

- Who else will you include in the evaluation?

- Who will you insist the prospect includes in the next steps?

- What's the prospect's compelling event?

- What criteria do you need to progress a prospect to the next stage?

- When will you establish the exact decision-making process of the prospect?

- What happens to their business if they take no action?

What role will influential stakeholders play in the decision-making process of your sales meeting?

- Who else should be included in your meeting?

- Who might have direct or indirect input on the decision?

- When will the prospect and their stakeholders get together to make the final decision?

Practice Paranoia in Sales— Nothing Is a Sure Thing

Healthy sales-cycle paranoia can be your best friend, since your prospect can always decide to go with the competition, opt to do nothing, or something could go wrong with the deal. Some people love surprises, but when it comes to the decision-making process, elite sales professionals don't. Finding out too late that the project and commercials need to be socialized with the board, that the founder has the final say, or that the prospect is ready to sign but can't proceed until the new budget is released next year are some surprises sales professionals hear all time.

Where does this project rank on the priority list? What is the compelling event? Why now? What happens if no decision is made? Why is this project important to internal stakeholders? Knowing who is making the decision, why they are making the decision, and when the decision is being made as early as possible improves the chances of success for the deal.

What is the prospect's decision-making process for the sales cycle?

- What people or resources will the prospect want to meet with to make a decision (e.g., a call with senior leadership, a reference call, or a call with customer support)?

- What is the real reason the prospect will want to speak with other resources in your business?

- When will you schedule the specific sessions during the sales cycle?

What is your decision-making process for the sales cycle?

- Who will you discuss the deal with in your business?

- Who else will you arrange to meet the prospect?

- Why will your sales cycle convince the prospect to choose you over the competition?

- When will the prospect meet their team and make a decision?

- What impact does the compelling event have on the decision?

- What is the impact if the prospect does nothing?

- What could go wrong to stop this deal from happening?

What is the decision-making process of influential stakeholders for the sales cycle?

- Who will have direct input on the decision, and who will have indirect influence?

- Why will decision influencers recommend your solution?

- When will the prospect and their stakeholders get together to make the final decision?

Better Decisions, a Better Plan, Better Outcomes

Some sales professionals create an annual sales plan themselves; others are mandated by their company to create one. Either way, the same principle of knowing the decision-making process applies. Who makes decisions? Why? And when? Putting our prospects front and center, we aspire to understand who the personas are that decide to buy, why they decide on vendors, and how far along in their sales process it is before they actively speak with sales. This gives us the ability to capture the attention of the right prospect at the right time. If we know this, then we can pitch to leadership for additional resources.

What is the decision-making process to determine the resources your sales attainment plan gets?

- What resources or support does your annual sales attainment plan require?

- Who will make the decision to give you resources or support? What impact will the decision have for them?

- What criteria will the decision makers use to make the decision of whether or not to support you?

- What exactly happens in the final moments of the decision-making process for resource requests, and how can you influence it?

What is the decision-making process for the targeted prospects of the sales attainment plan?

- Which personas typically make the decision to evaluate and buy your solutions?

- Why do prospects tend to do business with your company?

- In the buying process, when do prospects typically start speaking with sales?

**What is your decision-making
process for your sales attainment plan?**

- Who decides what part of the market to focus on?

- Why will prospects decide to proceed with you instead of others?

- When do typical decisions get made?

- What are typical compelling events?

It's Not about the Interview

Getting promoted is remarkably similar to closing a sale. For sales professionals, they are two sides of the same coin, although most can't see it.

A campaign to get promoted mirrors the sales cycle. We are always told to network for our next position. In sales, we meet the champion at the beginning of the sales cycle, qualify if our service is a fit for the prospect, and proceed to conduct discovery sessions to understand the exact outcome the prospect is working toward. We use those early sessions to understand what the prospect wants so we can paint a full picture of the value we will deliver.

When networking with hiring leaders, you are qualifying the opportunity. Acquiring more information from the hiring leader helps you decide if you actually want the job. Those early conversations are also a valuable opportunity to discover what the hiring leader wants from a new hire. The interview allows you to deliver your pitch, which should be customized around what the hiring leader wants. You can also arrange to share your interview pitch and approach with hiring leaders before the process starts. This is an opportunity to give hiring leaders a full picture of you and your capabilities.

Why work so hard to give your prospect a full picture of you and your solution in the sales cycle? Similarly, why give the hiring leaders a full picture of you when campaigning to gain promotion? When seeking promotion, why not just do the interview? Because the interview is not as important as you think. It is simply a means to get a full picture of you so a decision can be made.

Great sports teams and great sales teams handle the turn-over of team members in a similar way. Sports teams need a blend of young players breaking into the team, a core of players who deliver the required performances each week, and some older players who have great experience to share with others but will likely move on at the end of the year. A sales team full of extremely experienced older sales profession-als would be great for a year or two, but the business could lose the whole team in one go. Sports teams don't allow that to happen, and neither do great sales organizations. For this reason, sales leadership are often on the lookout for top tal-ent to nurture for a role on their team way in advance of the role becoming available. They know which team members are likely to move on soon, and they want to have options to replace them far in advance. For this reason, it's never too early to kick off a campaign to gain promotion. To increase your chances of success, it's important to know what the decision-making process for those involved in your potential promotion will be, why they are looking to promote, and how you might influence their decision ahead of the interview.

If you are campaigning for promotion, then the next few pages are gold dust for you. If you do nothing else, only this, then you'll have a phenomenal opportunity to get promoted. If you apply the thinking framework to the decision-making process involved in networking with hiring leaders, your interview, and your campaign for promotion, you'll have an edge over the competition.

Tactical Preparation for Networking with Leaders

Networking is defined as interacting with others to exchange information and develop professional contacts. This means you want to understand who makes and influences the final decision on hiring and ensure they are armed with information that clearly shows you're the best person for the job. Knowing who these people are, and why and when they are making their decision, is crucial to getting the right message to the right people at the right time to help them make the decision to hire you. Using your network to land messages indirectly via colleagues or mentors is another route to getting the right information to the decision makers.

What are leaders' decision-making processes for networking?

- Who do leaders decide to network with?

- Why do they choose to network?

- When and how do leaders like to network (e.g., virtually, in person, or at events; mornings or evenings)?

What is your decision-making process for networking with leaders who are hiring?

- Who specifically will you network with?

- Why will leaders choose to network with you? Apart from being a potential fit for their team, what additional value can you give them in the networking session itself?

- Why will the leader want to hire you after networking with you? What can you share that is unique?

- What are the three compelling reasons to hire you? (Make these points when networking, and reiterate them in your interview.)

When selecting people to network with, what is the decision-making process for stakeholders with influence over hiring leaders ?

- Who will have direct input on the hiring decision, and who will have indirect influence (e.g., offer recommendations to the hiring leader but not participate in the decision-making session)?

- When will the hiring leader and their stakeholders get together to make the final decision?

- Can you time a recommendation from an influential person just before the leaders are planning to make their decision?

Influence the Final Decision Meeting

Understanding how the interview is part of the decision-making process makes it easier to get hired. It's important to know who is ultimately making the decision and who influences the decision, including people who won't be in your interview. Are there certain criteria or is there a scoring rubric that must be followed? The more you know, the more you can improve your chances of being successful in the process.

What decision-making process does the interviewer have to use for the interview?

- Who is in your interview panel, and who has input on the hiring decision?

- Why might the interviewers *not* hire you?

- When will the decision makers make their decision?

What impact can you have on the decision-making process during the interview?

- Who is the ultimate decision maker you are trying to persuade to hire you, and what are their decision criteria?

- Why will the ultimate decision maker hire you ahead of the competition?

- When will they make a decision?

- What happens if they don't hire?

After the interview, who else can influence the hiring decision?

- Why will decision influencers recommend hiring you above the competition? What's their decision criteria?

- When will the hiring team get together to make the final decision?

US Presidents Need Eighty Million Supporters to Get the Job—You Need Just Three to Five

Getting a new job or a promotion depends on persuading multiple people that you are the best candidate. You can be clever about who you seek guidance and advice from when it comes to your campaign to gain promotion. The closer this person is to making the decision, the better.

As I've explained, most people focus all their energy on the interview. Instead, consider the decision-making process by finding out who will be in your interview panel and who will be in the room for the final decision. Make it a priority to network with all of them to understand their priorities and incorporate these into your interview presentation. This approach in itself will help you stand out from the crowd.

What is the exact decision-making process of the hiring team?

- What impact will the decision to campaign for promotion have on you?

- Who decides the criteria for promotion, and what is it? What *exactly* happens in the final moments of the decision-making process for the position, and how can you influence it?

What decision-making questions do elite sales professionals ask themselves when embarking on a promotion campaign?

- Who are the hiring leaders you'll network with?

- Why will the hiring leaders want to hire you?

- When will you kick off your campaign for promotion and start networking?

**What is the decision-making
process for leaders who are hiring?**

- Why are they looking for a new team member? Outside of
  the expected skills, what else can you bring to the team (e.g.,
  a talent for running events)?

- When are the decisions made about whom to interview?

- Who exactly will be making the decision on whom to hire,
  and when?

**What is the decision-making process for
stakeholders with influence over the leaders
who will make the hiring decision?**

- Who else typically has input on the decisions?

- When do influencers make recommendations to the hiring
  leaders?

CHAPTER SUMMARY

- Most people think the initial qualification call in prospecting,
  the demo in sales, and the job interview determine success
  or failure, but they don't; they are merely a single point of
  influence in a bigger decision-making process.

- Elite salespeople seek to understand all the points of influence in the decision-making process.

- Confirm the decision-making process at the beginning of selling and promotion-seeking activities.

- Constantly consider all possibilities, including what happens
  if they don't make a decision.

Chapter Questions for Hidden Habit #3:
What Is the Decision-Making Process?

Strategic Preparation:

- Who makes the decision?
- Why is the decision being made?
- When will the decision happen?

6

AN OVERLOOKED FUNDAMENTAL

Show Me You Know Me

Phil M. Jones

Nothing says you will listen to someone better than **sharing insights on something they didn't know you knew about them.**

PAUL M. CAFFREY

T HEIR PAST? *Their present? Their future?*

The individual? Their business? The wider environment?

By now you should be realizing from Paul's previous three chapters that although there is work to be done in getting ready for opportunities, the work before the work is entirely worth it. The current environment has pushed hard to dehumanize the sales process, and the result is that when an elite sales professional recognizes how to really add value, they soon find themselves as the *only* choice for their customer.

The world we now operate in is crowded with noise, full of promises to improve your efficiencies, and cluttered with insincere messaging, and with everybody so far stretched, convenience is the new luxury offering. The one true mainstay is that people buy people: people buy from people, people work for people, people solve other people's problems when things go wrong, and people want to celebrate with people when things go right. Couple this with Dale Carnegie's famous observation that you'll make more friends in a short period of time by showing genuine interest in other people than you will in a much longer time trying to get people interested in you. You can quickly be reminded that the people you are looking to influence are not interested in you and your offerings until you can prove that you are interested in them and theirs.

Historically, salespeople would make note of artifacts they witnessed in their prospects' offices and meeting rooms, pass comment on their clients' local hot spots, and use pre-meeting moments to make playful chitchat and try to create common ground. Sure, all these actions could add value to your conversation, but today they are hardly strategies or habits to rely on. I have repeatedly witnessed the carnage of a salesperson commenting on a family photo they've seen on a bookcase, only to then find out that the meeting is being conducted in a colleague's workspace, or assuming interest in "the game" last night just because the prospect lives in an area with a notable sports team, while the individual has no care or concern for the game. Lazy rapport still works—to a point. It's just that elite performers and genuine sales professionals choose to prepare everything and presume nothing.

With many meetings now being conducted remotely, and this medium looking like it's here for the long term, the importance of gaining a fair advantage with purposeful preparation is not just a good idea—it is, in fact, essential if you want to make each interaction really count. The currency of decision-making is trust. The sooner trust is established, the easier it becomes to move forward with momentum and the work before the work.

When COVID-19 hit big in March 2020, face-to-face meetings stopped overnight, and most people couldn't even go into their corporate offices, let alone meet customers. Instantly, every sales professional, entrepreneur, and business leader became "inside sales," and the genuine difficulties of what it took to build rapport over a video call were fast becoming a reality.

I recall that while working on this book, I spoke with Paul about a meeting he'd had with a vice president of a key account he'd just inherited. Early in the conversation, Paul had asked, "I'm guessing you didn't get to enter your new office?" A few weeks before the pandemic hit, the company had shared on social media that they had a new office. "Do you still use the office at the innovation science park? It's a beautiful coastal location." Then, switching gears, he asked for the VP's point of view on his industry and then offered up his own viewpoint. Paul went on to say that he'd seen the VP's interview at a large trade show recently, and he asked how the business would pivot, as trade shows would likely be canceled for the remainder of the year. This exchange ran for about five minutes, and it led to the discovery of a sales opportunity that closed a couple of months later. Through this conversation, Paul subtly demonstrated that knowing the person, business, and industry, while not talking about himself or his business, offered instant value to his new account.

Now more than ever, people want to have real conversations. Showing someone you know them, their business, and their industry at every point you connect with them gives them a genuine feeling of partnership. It shows that you have the emotional intelligence to see your role as a problem solver, and the more you can demonstrate true empathy, the more it becomes you and them versus the problems, as opposed to you versus them. Gone are the days of "winning the sale"—today's ambition from all parties should be to win together.

Meeting someone for the first time can be a little awkward. Sales professionals meet people in a manufactured environment, and both people are typically wondering what the other is looking to get out of the meeting. Prospects and customers are often guarded and fearful of being sold to, and the initial dialogue dictates much of how the rest of the engagement will play out. Conversations that lack flow and fail to become synchronized with all stakeholders can quickly run dry, and failure to find common ground damages your credibility and usefulness.

Peppering someone with random small talk or lazy general business questions is the fast lane to highlighting that you don't know enough about the person you're meeting, their business, and their industry. The moment you say, "Tell me a little about you and your business," you should not be surprised to see the other person roll their eyes as they realize they are entering into another pointless meeting.

Think of every exchange as a job interview. You have undoubtedly been conditioned to know that if you want to be hired in a new role, the more you do your homework, the more likely you are to position your skills and experience to the precise needs of the role. Every sales appointment is just another interview, and if you really want to win the opportunity, showing them that you know them is really just table stakes.

The work involved in getting to a position of confidence in this area is not always easy, but it's almost always worth it. Years ago it would have required a private investigation team to collect the required intelligence, but now almost everything you need is readily available, should you choose to look for it.

Minimum standards for prospecting, progressing accounts, and promotion opportunities would be:

- Reviewing corporate websites, search engines, and news updates prior to each conversation

- Subscribing to the newsletters of the people/businesses you are looking to influence

- Actively following the social channels of the people who matter

- Considering wider industry trends that are affecting their focus at this time

- Understanding their culture so you can meet them where they are at

More evolved preparedness comes from

- sending meaningful agendas ahead of discussions/meetings;
- knowing what to wear to fit into their culture environment;
- reviewing shared contacts to help showcase a shared network;
- adding personalization to any supporting documents or presentations; and
- preparing questions to show that you have the pulse on their current reality.

Elite sales professionals will always

- understand any potential objections or points of frustration prior to the discussion;
- see bigger opportunities than those that currently exist;
- prepare questions that bring clarity to those opportunities;
- research case studies and other names that can be used as evidence to support any proposals they are looking to make;
- share relevant and valuable articles and information with their customers and prospects; and
- actively look to make useful connections and new business opportunities for others.

Showing a person that you know them early in a conversation causes the other person to light up and feel valued, which instantly amplifies rapport. You get to see a glimmer of the real person, and they become so much more interested in you and the conversation. A small comment about something you have never discussed—like "How is the new office?" or "Congratulations on the recent award," or even thanking them for their insights in a recent article they published—makes them realize you have done your homework. What's more, it shows them you want this, and people love to be wanted. This is the work that moves you from being a valued vendor to being a trusted partner.

Elevating yourself to this trusted partner status means communicating in very different ways. Sure, knowing your company, products, services, and pricing is all entirely necessary, but when you can dial up your genuine knowledge of the other person, you can unlock the gateway to the true sphere of influence. In my experience, there are four keys that unlock this position better than any others:

Genuine praise: Take a moment to show someone that you are entirely impressed by an action they have taken or an outcome they have achieved.

The request of their opinion: Make a specific ask of someone who is important to you or your industry because you truly value their point of view.

Sincere gratitude: Thank them for something truly meaningful that exists only because of their contribution.

A privileged invitation: Ask them to be part of something that demonstrates and recognizes a desire for their company, experience, or expertise.

When the "Show Me You Know Me" button is pressed, the person you are meeting leans forward in their chair and starts to look forward to the rest of the conversation. Drop a little more knowledge about their business and industry, and it will show you are a sales professional who may have valuable ideas and insight. Ultimately, execs are looking to repack your knowledge and insight as their own to bring value to their business and improve it. It's possible to elevate a routine sales conversation into a value-filled business conversation focused on growing the business as the exec recognizes that your ideas or insight could be very helpful to their organization.

Ask Yourself: Can I Show Them That I Know Them?

There are three levels to showing a prospect or customer that you know them: the individual, the business, and the wider environment.

Let's take the scenario of speaking to a prospect for the first time. Their guard may be a little higher since you are a sales professional trying to sell something.

For the *individual*, answer the following questions:

Their Past

- Where did they work before? What qualifications do they have?

- What content (interviews, podcasts, articles, social media posts, etc.) on them is available?

- Has the individual spoken with your company before? Check the CRM (Customer Relationship Management)!

Their Present

- How long have they been in the role?

- What LinkedIn contacts do you share?

- What groups and influencers do they follow? What is their recent activity? What are they saying on social media, from a business perspective?

Their Future

- What is their likely motivation?

- Compared with others, what is likely to be the next role for them?

Their Personal Interests
By checking their social media profiles, can you determine their

- family situation,
- sports,
- hobbies, and
- other interests?

Even if you have no experience of their hobby, you can call that out and speak to them in more detail about it by using a beginner's mindset of curiosity.

For the *business*, answer the following questions:

The Business's Past

- Has someone else from the business evaluated your solutions before? (Check the CRM!)

- Look at their products and services and their value proposition.

- Review their case studies. Are there any mutual customers?

- What is the history of the business, and what is the health of their financial statements?

The Business's Present

- What can you learn from their company press releases and news page?

- What other articles can you find from search engines?

- What are they posting on social media?

- What is the current organizational chart and potential decision-making process?

- What are the current cultural focuses inside the organization?

- How involved are they in philanthropic work?

- Who are their top three competitors? What's on the competitors' PR and news pages?

- What do employees say about their experience working there?

- Is the company hiring?

- Has there been any investment?

- Has there been a change in the C-suite?

- Who do they currently partner with?

The Business's Future

- What comments has the CEO or leadership made about the future of the business?

- What predictions can you make about the future of their place in the industry?

For the *wider environment,* answer the following questions:

The Wider Environment

- What other companies in their industry with similar size and location (the closer the better) are using your solution?

- Are there case studies and testimonials that may be relevant?

- Who are the main players in the industry?

- What are the industry trends? (Tip: Google the industry with the term "trends [current year].pdf"—e.g., "AI trends 2022.pdf.")

Create a Fair Advantage

Showing a prospect, customer, or even hiring leader that you know them is the one area that is in your complete control and delivers you a fair advantage for outperforming the competition. Making these steps habitual and valuing the preparation involved is testimony to you respecting the time and attention of the other person or people and means you are fully aware that your role is to make their life better, not to achieve your objective. Achieving mastery in this area means genuinely caring about other people and looking to understand them, their current situation, and any other external factors ahead of any interaction, which allows you to make more of your conversations really count.

CHAPTER SUMMARY

- People you're looking to influence are not interested in you and your offerings until you can prove that you are interested in them and theirs.

- Elite performers prepare everything and presume nothing.

- Early in conversations, with prepared comments or questions, subtly captivate people by showing you made the effort to understand what's important in their world.

- Elite sales professionals see bigger opportunities than those that currently exist and act on them.

Chapter Questions for An Overlooked Fundamental: Can I Show Them I Know Them?

Strategic Preparation:

- Can I show them I know them individually, know their business, and know the wider environment?

- Can I show them that I know their past, present, and future ambitions?

7

How Will You Achieve This?

Paul M. Caffrey

Optimism without realism is simply hope. **Elite performers never rely on hope.**

PHIL M. JONES

UILD THE team? Set the expectation? Remove friction?
Imagine you and your closest friends are at a crowded, trendy rooftop bar. Tipping the server generously will encourage him to come back on time for the next order of drinks. Setting expectations with the server and asking him to come back for the next order in thirty minutes will mean you can concentrate on talking with friends rather than spending five minutes trying to get his attention. You can take this a step further and order the signature cocktail for everyone. This removes the friction of a complex order and means a single nod to "Same again?" will keep the good times rolling.

Generously tipping the server also opens the door to a whole world of possibilities that can make your evening even better. When you're ready for dinner, you can ask the server to get you a table with the best views of the city. Maybe there is something one of your friends wants to order that's not on the menu—you can request it. In some ways you and the server have become a team, offering your friends a first-class experience on this night out. You can't always give your friends a premium experience on your own, but teaming up with the server is an example of how you can give yourself a fair advantage.

Imagine that while enjoying the great views, you and your friends are starving! Then it takes forty minutes for the food to be served, as the restaurant is so busy. Your friends are probably annoyed and frustrated by having to wait so long for the food! Let's rewind the experience and imagine the situation if the server set the right expectation.

Suppose you ask what the waiting time is for food and the server explains that there is a forty-minute wait due to the restaurant being so busy, but that the kitchen is Michelin-starred, so the food will be amazing. This gives you the opportunity to order some appetizers and removes the frustration that builds when you're hungry and don't know when your food will arrive. In this scenario, with the server setting the expectation of the wait, what would your friends say? Most likely they would say the food was sublime and worth the wait, and that the place was busy, but the service was great.

On a day-to-day basis, you might be targeted to find opportunities to pass to the sales team. How are you going to achieve this? Well, beyond the obvious tasks to try and reach prospects, could you build a team to help with this? When something works well for you, can you share it with your colleagues? Can you give them value and earn the right to ask them questions when you come across an objection or a request that is unusual? Maybe a colleague isn't in the same role as you; perhaps they are in marketing, but they might still be able to help you, and the insight of what is working for you might help their future marketing efforts too.

If you're qualifying an opportunity, can you set clear expectations with the prospect and the sales team about what to expect from the next call, in which you introduce them to each other? If you are targeted to find leads for the sales team that they then have to qualify into the active pipeline for you to hit your target, can you speak with the sales team and get a clear understanding of exactly what information they are looking for to progress leads to opportunities? Can you make a concerted effort to capture the information to remove friction from the leads that you pass to the sales team?

In sales, it's important to realize that you can't always achieve a sale on your own. You may be able to sell, but you may also require a wider team to bring more value to increase the deal size and get it closed faster. Lewis Hamilton has won the Formula One world championship many times, and his Mercedes team can change his tires in 1.8 seconds. However, while cruising on the highway in his electric Mercedes EQC, Hamilton suffered a blowout and had to get his hands dirty, like the pit lane mechanics, to change the tire himself, which took longer than a couple of seconds. Hamilton is a great driver, but he's much faster when he has a team to help him.

Having a team you can rely on is especially important in high-stakes situations. With just a few weeks remaining in the fiscal year, a CEO agreed to evaluate new software and sign off by year-end, since he needed a solution implemented for the start of the following year. This brought a feeling of dread to the sales professional, Camila, since she knew timelines were very tight for completing an evaluation. When she shared the evaluation plan with the solution engineer, implementation partner, and senior executive, Camila was delighted to discover that she had built up enough goodwill throughout the year that they all went the extra mile to give the prospect a premium sales cycle experience.

Explaining in advance that because it was the last few weeks of the fiscal year some calls would need to be early in the morning or late in the evening, Camila set expectations with the CEO and his team to allow more flexibility. It's much better than saying the day before that the next meeting must be at 8:00 a.m. or 5:00 p.m. the next day. Knowing well ahead of time to expect this meant the CEO and his team could plan their day so that early or late sessions were less inconvenient.

To remove friction for the CEO and mitigate the chances of running out of time to get the deal completed, Camila scheduled paperwork that was usually reviewed at the end of a sales cycle—such as the master services agreement, the security and compliance of the platform, and the scoping of the implementation—to be agreed on earlier in the evaluation process. This meant that there were fewer hurdles to overcome at the end of the process.

By building a team, setting expectations, and removing friction, Camila built on the goodwill she had generated with her colleagues to give the prospect a premium sales experience. Her preparation gave her the ability to execute her vision by leveraging the fair advantage she gave herself.

Don't Just Set Expectations with Prospects

You may have resource challenges that affect your prospecting: you may not have a sales development resource aligned directly with you, the sales development team might be split among you and a number of your colleagues, or perhaps they react only to inbound inquiries and qualify them for the sales team. Getting access to resources to do a prospecting campaign could be very challenging. Perhaps you are busy and don't have the time to prospect on a consistent basis yourself—it's no surprise we can't advocate this!

If your organization doesn't have sales development, it's critical that prospecting is built into the daily routine of sales professionals. When your organization does have sales development, sales professionals need to optimize the time they spend prospecting to concentrate on high payoff accounts and ensure they also give themselves enough time to sell. When sales professionals can't carve out time to prospect, and business development representatives are not working their patch either, the lead flow dries up.

It doesn't matter how good marketing events are if you don't have prospects to attend them. Without invitations, marketing events become more missed opportunities for new leads. If your business hosts marketing events, supporting them means more resources get allocated to running events, which can be great at removing friction on deals toward the end of the sales cycle. Depending on your business and industry, these "small" events can generate a lot of income.

You need to put together a team, set targets so everyone is clear on what's expected of them, and make it easy for the team to participate in the prospecting campaign. An account team gets better results than people operating independently. However, clarity and expectations are important: ambiguity can hamper prospecting, and a lack of understanding of what's expected in follow-up contributes to poor prospecting results.

When prospecting, there is great comfort in knowing that the full resources of the business are available to support you in creating the opportunity. It makes the outreach and qualification sessions with the customer much more engaging, enjoyable, and, importantly, valuable to them. The admin work in preparation for prospecting activities and following up qualification calls is greatly reduced when clear requirements and instructions are shared.

Your business will likely have a prospecting playbook. The good news is that the following thinking framework can be applied to improve its results. You can mastermind prospecting and outsource a significant chunk of it to other resources.

You can get yourself into the position of being chased by sales or business development representatives wanting to actively prospect into your accounts. When your prospecting process becomes a finely tuned machine, customers have valuable and engaging conversations with sales development reps that create new opportunities. A prospecting system that works creates a steady lead flow.

Returning to our prospecting scenarios, it's time to start working on how you are actually going to achieve your prospecting goals. Let's see how you will prospect better with cold outreach, qualification calls, and prospecting campaigns.

What Value Does Your Cold Outreach Offer to Prospects?

Cold outreach is the least glamourous part of sales, but it's one of the most important to keep your pipeline healthy. Who can you get on board to help? If you are in business development or sales, can you team up to work on a targeted outbound campaign? Can partners gain revenue from working with you? Can they team up for business generation too?

How can you make it as easy as possible to do cold outreach? How can you set the expectations of prospects about the value of speaking with you? How can you make it easier for the prospect to act and book an appointment? You have just seconds to prompt a prospect to react. Asking for a time to speak with them is so vague that it promotes inaction, so offering a ten-minute call at a specific time often makes them more likely to speak with you.

How will prospects achieve
success responding to cold outreach?

- If the prospect doesn't respond to cold outreach, do they have a team that will benefit from your solution? If so, who could you target?

- What value can the prospects expect if they respond?

How will you achieve success with cold outreach?

- Who will you target, and how will your solution increase their success?

- How often will you create and send messages?

- How will you remove friction and make it super easy to respond?

Who Attends Your Qualification Calls, and What Do They Expect?

Who else should attend the qualification call? Are decision makers booked to attend the call? If not, should you ask them to join? How can you align expectations before the call? (What if the prospect is expecting a demo, but you're just planning to discuss their needs?)

People don't like change, and a lot of people don't like salespeople. Considering we are selling change, expecting friction becomes the default setting. What insight can you share with the prospect? What key questions to disrupt the status quo can you prepare? What industry point of view can you share that makes considering change a must? The outcome is to determine if the prospect is a fit for your service, and if they are, then you're selling the next steps, which most likely involve completing a full evaluation of your services.

How will prospects achieve success from qualification calls?

- Can prospects get their wider team available for the first call?

- Can you clarify the prospect's expectation for the qualification call?

- What can you do to remove friction and make qualification calls better for prospects?

How will you achieve success with your qualification calls?

- Who's needed on your team, and what information is required to qualify the opportunity?

- What expectations will you set with the prospect for the qualification call and next steps?

- How will you remove friction? How will you prepare questions for the calls?

Do Your Prospecting Campaigns Include Calls and Collaboration?

The prospecting efforts get real once you have the team in place and expectations are set. Who else will help you prospect? If you use partners, are they open to joint prospecting for new business? If your business has sales development, business development reps, or product-specific salespeople within the business, will you ask them to help if their targets benefit from collaborative deals?

Having your resources in place, you can decide who from your team prospects into which persona. For example, the sales development rep might target the director level in an account, and you as the sales professional might target the CEO.

It's the cadences and sequences that make prospecting so effective, and the phone is the secret weapon that supersedes the sequences and cadences! Setting clear expectations on the type of outbound activity and the time of the outbound activity in a coordinated way drives success. Including calls throughout your prospecting sequences is great because when you speak with a prospect, you can confirm their interest and book a meeting or confirm their lack of interest and remove them from your sequence much faster. Once a meeting is booked or a prospect confirms they are not interested, they are removed from the prospecting list and replaced by another business to target. If you routinely prospect ten companies at a time, this ensures you're always prospecting ten companies.

**How will your previous experience
improve this prospecting campaign?**

- What additional knowledge, skills, or resources will you require to achieve a successful prospecting campaign?

- How exactly will you go from where you are today to your best possible outcome?

- What do you need to change to achieve this?

- What do you need to start doing, stop doing, and continue doing?

**How will targeted prospects of the
prospecting campaign achieve success?**

- How will the prospects have more success with your
  solution?

**How will you achieve success
with the prospecting campaign?**

- Who can you add to your team to achieve success with this
  prospecting campaign?

- What expectations (call to action) will you set with the
  prospect?

- How will you remove friction for the prospect to respond?

**How will influential stakeholders help you
achieve success with the prospecting campaign?**

- Is there an opportunity to leverage a relationship one of
  your executives has with an equivalent executive in the prospect's company?

Setting Your Teammates up for Sales Success

One of the most frustrating problems in sales is being unable to
secure people and resources to help run a customer evaluation.
When a sales cycle lacks either, it gets delayed, and as we all
know, time kills deals. Be wary of rushing to create the resources
yourself; not only do you waste time and effort, but you also
often offer an inferior customer experience. Tweaking existing
resources is a better track to take. If you do manage to secure
someone to help—such as a solution engineer or partner—
make it a priority to brief them in advance. Sometimes new

people entering a deal ask the prospect repetitive questions, and it can feel like they are being "requalified" or that the sales-person didn't listen to them during the initial call. New people supporting the deal without adequate time to prepare often miss the important nuances of the customer's requirements and provide a bad customer experience.

When supporting material (such as custom pitch decks and commercial presentations) isn't ready for the customer, it means the sales professional must talk the customer through the offer instead. This makes it much more difficult for custom-ers to take on the information and very challenging for them to present it back internally. A lack of digital resources for pre-sentations and follow-up worsen the customer experience and reduce the likelihood of winning the business.

It's possible to get support from solution engineers, co-primes, partners, and first-line, second-line, and even third-line leaders at short notice. It is also possible to provide notes to solution engineers, a solution plan to partners, and an exec briefing to leadership that makes you a pleasure to work with and impresses prospects, as they aren't repeating them-selves each time. You can have personalized content that you can deliver and follow up with quickly. It's possible to gain a reputation as someone who is meticulous in preparation and masterful in execution.

You can also have a plan for achieving a closed deal on a sales cycle that includes executive alignment as part of the sales team. This alignment can help to grow the size of the deal and also reduce friction in the sign-off process. When a member of the C-suite feels they are connected with a true counterpart, it eases the negotiation process.

The payoff from securing resources for sales meetings at the right time is that prospects you onboard or upsell/cross-sell become advocates that become valuable references for future customers. Repeatable templates that you create in your own style give you the ability to follow up fast with top-class information. Since speed is everything in sales, getting excellent, personalized resources and support when you need them is critical, but it comes from building up a reputation for being respectful and prepared. We'll consider next how to prepare for your sales activities by asking how you can achieve success through building a team, setting expectations, and removing friction.

Preparing for Great Sales Meetings

Prospects have much better experiences in sales meetings when they include all the relevant people from their organization, have clear expectations, and work openly with the sales professional. We can encourage this behavior with conversations in advance, agendas shared ahead of time, and seeking clarification on what the prospect wants to add to the agenda before the sales meeting. This creates focused meetings with better outcomes.

Setting clear expectations for colleagues and partners supporting you is also essential to a successful meeting. Often, follow-up is promised throughout the meeting. Keeping a close eye on this and making sure it happens reflects very well on you. When multiple people attend a meeting, individual follow-up will get a much higher response rate!

How will prospects achieve success in your sales meetings?

- Which members of the prospect's team should they include in sales meetings?

- What is the prospect's expectation for your sales meeting?

- What friction can you remove from the sales meeting to make it more valuable?

How will you achieve success in the sales meeting?

- Who's needed on your team to achieve success in the sales meeting?

- What expectations will you set with the prospect?

- How will you remove friction for the sales meeting in order to progress it?

How will you utilize influential stakeholders to achieve success in the sales meeting?

- Can you have a member of your leadership team join an early-stage sales meeting to remove friction early in case you get to a difficult negotiation later?

Making It Easy for the CEO to Sign Off

To achieve anything meaningful, you need the right people. Start with who is required on your side and the prospect's side and who else is required in your sales cycle team (such as partners) to make the dream a reality.

What else is needed to achieve a successful sales cycle? What expectations need to be set internally and externally? What can you do to canvas the members of the customer's evaluation team to establish where they stand today, and what will it take to get them shouting at their CEO to procure your service? Our role as elite sales professionals is to win over the evaluation team so that they ask their CEO to buy. It's much more difficult for a CEO to sign off on a project when their team isn't convinced, even when the CEO wants the solution.

How will prospects achieve success throughout the sales cycle?

- Who else from the organization will the prospect include in the evaluation?

- What is the prospect's expectation for your sales cycle?

- How can you remove friction for the prospect throughout the sales cycle?

How will you achieve success throughout the sales cycle?

- Who's needed on your team to achieve success in the sales cycle?

- What expectations will you set with the prospect?

- How will you remove friction from the sales cycle in order to progress?

How will influential stakeholders help you achieve success during the sales cycle?

- How can you leverage your leadership team to get involved early in the sales cycle to help win the business later in the sales cycle?

- What expectations will you set with your leadership team?

Consider Everyone's Goals

It's important to have a sharp vision of how you will execute your sales attainment plan, because sales is a full-on, busy profession. Who is in the wider team that will help you make your annual sales plan a reality? Are some aligned with you already? Are others more difficult to get? What is the most effective team you can put together?

Teamwork is essential for sustained sales success, with each contributor having personal motivations. This is even more challenging when each person is targeted differently by the business (e.g., different success metrics for presales, onboarding, and support). Individuals on each team don't always have to work together, and they can say no to supporting the sales professional. Typically, sales development reps are working toward being sales professionals (account executives—AEs), and solution engineers can be motivated by working on interesting projects or even an opportunity to improve their close rate stats too. A wonderful way to maintain the motivation of team members supporting your sales attainment plan is to understand their goals for the year and factor in helping them get there with your plan. For a sales development rep, you can set the expectation of the prospecting to be completed and offer for them to ride shotgun on a deal so they can use the experience for their progression. As we look at the value a project offers a customer, let's also consider the value that working on a project offers someone helping us, such as a solution engineer, and articulate this in a way that reduces the possibility of pushback to work with you.

How will your previous experience improve your sales attainment plan?

- How will you accomplish success with this sales attainment plan?

- What, if any, additional knowledge, skills, or resources will you need to achieve a successful sales attainment plan?

- Who's needed on your team to achieve success with this sales attainment plan?

- What exact steps will you take to create your best possible outcome?

- What do you need to start, stop, and continue doing?

How will you achieve success with the sales attainment plan for everyone else?

- How can you leverage your leadership team for prospecting or challenging negotiations?

- What expectations will you set with your team?

- How can you remove friction for leadership when they engage with one of your prospects?

Make Yourself an Easy Hire

Sales professionals are sometimes unaware of how open senior leaders in the business are to mentoring and sponsoring people through the promotion and interview process. They don't realize guidance is available from senior leadership and don't even ask. Getting time with these influential people is a great opportunity to set their expectations about you and your career. It puts you on the radar as someone who could be useful to them at some point in the future. Personal development removes friction for hiring leaders to pick you for the role because it helps you meet the specific requirements for certain job titles. Many sales professionals are unaware of the internal resources, training, and courses available, not to mention whether they can use an education budget (sometimes up to $5,000 per year). If they do have a budget, most don't know what to spend it on!

Other sales professionals don't put a personal development plan in place to get better and ready for the next role. If they do know of resources, they are often common ones, such as a pitch deck with specific key points to hit for interviews, which can restrict them from standing out. Being unaware of the wider resources available stifles your innovation. If you show little to no innovation, your presentations will be boring and forgettable and will get lost in the crowd. This cohort of sales professionals tends to compare their sales performance to that of the successfully promoted and wonder why the others are promoted above them. The sales professionals who don't take action and run a campaign to get promoted tend to spend a few extra years in each role. They either ignore or are not aware of the campaign for promotion that successful candidates undertake to remove any friction that might prevent hiring leaders from choosing them.

However, many sales professionals all over the world get senior leadership to mentor and sponsor them through the promotion process for exciting new roles. They have personal development plans that are structured over the course of the year to prepare them for the next position, and they take full advantage of resources such as online training, internal courses, and an education fund when available. There are sales professionals looking for innovative ways to stand out in their interviews. Maybe they use videos featuring colleagues, customers, and partners instead of a dull "about me" page, for instance. These are the people you are up against: people who are serious about getting promoted and think long and hard about how they are going to achieve the promotion. They realize that promotion is based not on a meritocracy and a single interview, but on who shows themselves as the best candidate over a long period of time.

Liaising with senior management for mentorship and sponsorship is really powerful because it builds your brand and increases the likelihood of the hiring leader getting a recommendation to hire you. A single sentence from the right person to the hiring leader can make all the difference, but ultimately you want to build a boardroom of influencers. Mentorship and sponsorship (if you can get it) will have interviewers leaning forward in their chairs. Interviewers will want to know more about how you secured the impressive mentor and will be very interested in the wisdom you gained and how it will help you in the next role. It also says that this is not just a job for you but a career, and it creates an air of impressive professionalism that will stay with you throughout the interview. The interviewers will be excited by action you could take in the role and what insight you could bring to their team, and you'll be a frontrunner for the position you are going for. There is nothing better than seeing an engaged interview team in front of you and knowing they are thinking, *I'm going to hire this person.*

Even if you're not going for promotion this year, like the most successful sales professionals, you should always have a personal development plan—a framework to help you identify and improve strengths and weaknesses to achieve specific aims or goals over the short, medium, and long term. An ongoing personal development plan focused on your career will help you make the most of opportunities as they arise.

When interviews come along, an ongoing personal development plan will give you the confidence to highlight your awareness of your weaknesses as well as your willingness to take action to improve them. Challenging yourself and executing an innovative interview presentation is also a great way to increase the skills in your repertoire. You can always improve presentation and persuasion skills. Delivering an exciting and innovative presentation built on your personal development will make the experience stand out for the interview panel.

Let's look at how you can achieve success in your career promotion activities by building a team, setting expectations, and removing friction.

Fearless Networking

There are many aspects to networking, but being brave when deciding whom to network with and offering a clear message are two important ways to achieve success.

Being brave with the people you aspire to network with will definitely help your cause. The more senior the influencer, the more likely their recommendation will help get you hired. Consider whom you should network with and aim higher! It's also important to speak to those directly involved in the decision. What might be your strategic approach to building the team of people you will network with?

It's also worth considering the value you can bring to a networking conversation. Put yourself in their shoes, and consider how you can remove any friction that may prevent them from hiring you. Can you provide three memorable messages that will make it easy for the hiring leader to know what you'll achieve if you get the role?

How will leaders achieve success networking with potential candidates?

- Do leaders consult their network to get opinions on candidates prior to networking with candidates? What will your former leaders and colleagues say about you?

- What are the hiring leaders' expectations for their networking meetings?

- How might leaders remove friction early in the conversation for candidates they network with? (Look out for a comment early in the discussion to put you at ease.)

How will you achieve success in networking with hiring leaders?

- Who in your network has the respect of the hiring leader and can recommend they meet with you?

- What expectations will you set with leaders when you network with them?

- How can you remove friction early in the conversation for leaders networking with you?

Is There an Interview Rubric?

Interviewing is a solo task, but preparing for interviews is a team sport on both sides of the fence. Who could help you prepare: colleagues, people on the sales team you are aspiring to join, the hiring leader, maybe decision influencers? That's right—the interviewer will have a team of people helping them decide if they should hire you. What could you do in advance to build a team to help you achieve the goal of being hired, drawing on both your peers and the hiring team?

What messaging could you share to set the expectations of what you will bring to the role? If you are asking people to endorse you, what specific messages will you ask them to share, and when and how will they do this for you? How could you make this easier for them—could you share specific bullet points, or find a time or an event that works for them to have a chat? What is the extra mile you'll need to go to ensure you have removed any friction that might prevent this conversation from happening?

How will your interviewer achieve success in the interview?

- Does the interviewer require a wider team to evaluate your candidacy? Who?

- What is the interviewer's expectation for your interview? Is there an official scorecard/rubric the interviewer is mandated to use?

How will you achieve success in your interview?

- Who on the interview panel can you get on your team to advocate for hiring you, even before the interview?

- What expectations can you set at the beginning of your interview to make it easier for the panel to get what they need and understand why they should hire you?

**How will influential stakeholders help
you achieve success with the interview?**

- Can you get a stakeholder who has influence with your interview panel to recommend you after the interview is finished but before their final decision is made?

- How can you leverage your existing leadership team to be successful in the interview?

Strategic Networking to Build Your Personal Brand

Having a team of influential stakeholders of varying ranks of superiority recommending you will vastly improve your chances of getting promoted. This powerful team will not just land in your lap—it needs to be built. It can consist of your leadership team, future peers, mentors, colleagues, customers, and, most importantly, people who are hiring! Leaders who receive a recommendation of a specific candidate from someone they respect recognize the effort and talents of the candidate to get that message to land at the right time. It reduces the risk in hiring and sets the candidate apart from the pack as someone who knows what they are doing and can get something important done.

**How will your previous experience
improve your promotion campaign?**

- What steps will you take to go from where you are today to your best possible outcome?

- What do you need to start, stop, and continue doing in order to achieve this?

How will the hiring leader achieve success?

- Who is involved with helping the hiring leader make a decision?

- What does the hiring leader expect from them, and how can you wildly exceed these expectations?

- How can you remove the usual friction in a promotion campaign and make it really easy for the leaders to offer you the position?

**How will you achieve success
with your promotion campaign?**

- How will you build relationships with the hiring leaders?

- What expectations can you set in advance with the leadership team about the specific impact you'll have in the role?

- How will you remove friction for the hiring team to hire you?

**How will influential stakeholders help you
achieve success with your campaign for promotion?**

- How will you build a team of influential stakeholders who will advocate for you as the right hire? What expectations will you set with your leadership team to get them on board with supporting and recommending you for your next role?

- What can you do in advance from a development perspective to remove friction for the hiring leader so they will offer you the position (e.g., working with bigger accounts for the first time or moving into a role where you will have to interview and hire people yourself; can you shadow someone already doing the role ahead of your interview)?

CHAPTER SUMMARY

- Setting and communicating clear expectations is essential when working with people who don't work for you.

- Sometimes prospects have defined decision criteria, and sometimes interviewers have a scoring rubric. Factor this into your thinking when making your plan.

- Mentors, sponsors, and education help remove friction when going for promotion. Elite salespeople never waste resources (e.g., education benefits are always used).

- Be fearless when networking; decide whom you should network with and then aim a level higher.

**Chapter Questions for Hidden Habit #4:
How Will You Achieve This?**

Strategic Preparation:

- How will you build the team?
- How will you set expectations?
- How will you remove friction?

8

HIDDEN HABIT #5

How Will You Progress the Desired Outcome?

Paul M. Caffrey

You can always achieve more with less when you do the work to remove the obstacles.

PHIL M. JONES

POSSIBLE OBSTACLES? *Shared road map? Confirmed commitment?*

Progressing a deal to a desired outcome is a lot like dating. Let's imagine you're on a date. The conversation is good and you're both getting on well. You have a lot in common, and you think this could go somewhere. After a few more dates, you start thinking, *What do I want to happen next?* You decide you might want to get into a relationship.

What are the obstacles that might stand in your way? Some are a little more immediate, like where you both live. Are you in the same city? If not, who will move, and will you move in together? Or will you agree to live in separate cities and travel for the initial period of the relationship? What hours do you work: Are you both nine-to-five, or does one of you work the weekends? Will you get enough time to see each other?

Broadly speaking, are you on the same trajectory? Have you both committed to the idea? What does an ideal day look like for both of you? Do you both want to get married? Have kids? Having a shared road map early can mitigate big problems later. Plans can always change, but if one person wants kids and the other person doesn't, then that could be a deal breaker down the line.

When thinking about how we will progress to a desired outcome, we are building a shared road map, sometimes better known as a mutual plan—an agreed-upon set of actions that are cocreated and co-owned by the sales professional and their prospect to achieve a defined goal written in the words of the prospect. Mutual plans with compelling events defined by a problem that must be solved by a certain date to prevent an executive or the business suffering consequences have more successful outcomes.

Deals without shared road maps often result in sales professionals providing demos and information, wasting time and other resources, with an assumed or soft close date. Unstructured sales cycles fuel indecision, the mortal enemy of sales professionals. We can all agree that indecision is worse than a "no" for so many reasons.

Knowing how prospects will progress to their desired outcomes makes it easier to run more deals side by side, and it increases deal values too. This maximizes the return for your time. However, running large deal evaluations side by side can create pressure situations. I once witnessed a sales professional orchestrating a four-hour demo playback to the leadership team of one prospect on-site and then racing across the road to a hotel lobby to run a commercial presentation with the chairman of another business for another large deal. In that scenario, both deals had a shared road map with possible obstacles called out, and both had confirmed commitment on decisions by specific dates. The road maps were shared with the prospects at the beginning and end of each meeting to confirm that both parties were working to the same timelines. Having a clear plan to work toward made it easier for the different stakeholders of each business to get involved when they were required, and it made it easier to get both deals closed.

Typically there is some point of urgency: a customer requires the project to be live for a business impacting reason, or perhaps it's a manufactured urgency, via end-of-quarter/ end-of-year discounting, that is pushing it forward. The latter is an approach we want to avoid: the purpose of a discount is to accelerate a decision, but it can have the opposite effect by training customers to wait for important deadlines like the end of a quarter or year.

Most sales professionals tend to put a few days or a week between each meeting due to not having an agreed-upon plan. Some who have a shared road map leave a week between sessions, as it feels like a natural gap to offer. It's understandable, because sales professionals are all competing to get time in our customers' diaries, and we are trying to secure our own internal resources, such as solution engineers for demos. It takes time to prepare presentations, demos, and commercials. However, this should be reduced to the shortest amount of time possible.

An experiment was conducted with two customers with deals in the pipeline. Both deals were transformational, although they were average-sized deals with standard requirements. Instead of setting a typical four-to-six-week shared road map, both were presented with a ten-day shared road map. Surprisingly, both customers worked toward the deadline and both deals closed. Why did it work? Well, the shared road map made it easy for the customers to understand the evaluation process. The shorter time period helped build momentum and focused the minds of both the sales professionals and the prospects. Booking the meetings into the diary in advance also helped ensure the customers had the time to attend the key sessions and make a decision.

What does this mean for sales professionals? We can progress the desired outcome with a shared road map agreed on by sales professionals and prospects, no matter how big or small the deals are, because the shared road map accelerates sales evaluations, helps qualify how real the deals are, and gives more time to close even more business.

It's important to remember that although many prospects consider sales to be problem-solving, your experience and insight can also help you find potential problems. As you'll most likely be speaking to prospects as part of a shared road map, make sure problem-finding conversations don't stray from the purpose of the meeting you are running.

Keeping meetings and sessions on time is always a challenge, but it's critical to success. If you are in a sales meeting that's booked for one hour with a full agenda (e.g., introduction, presentation, demo, questions, and next steps), sometimes part of the meeting will run over time. Let's imagine the demo is fascinating for the customer and that part of the meeting takes more time than allotted to it. Make sure that ten minutes before the end, alarm bells go off in your head and you confirm the next steps on the shared road map, even if you're not going to finish the current session: "We are running tight on time, and it feels like we are going to cover what you need. As we have ten minutes left, I want to check that we are still on track for the next session. Also, how do you want to spend these last ten minutes?" It's also a good idea to check if the prospect has time to stay on the call past when it's scheduled to finish. If the senior decision maker is leaving a meeting early, stop and thank them for attending and explain the next steps the session is working toward. A real ninja trick is to share the details, time, and date for the next session the senior decision maker will be involved in, as it makes you look very sharp as a sales professional. People want to do business with people who are on their game.

Knowing the possible obstacles, having a shared road map, and confirming commitment means you will progress more prospects to their desired outcome, giving you a fair advantage.

Once They See It, They Can't Unsee It

Prospecting to customers without a specific plan leads to inter-
mittent prospecting, which is the most ineffective form. The
odds of being lucky enough to reach a prospect with one communication just as they have a need and them responding to
just one message are very low. Sometimes marketing sends a
communication, sales professionals reach out randomly, and
business development might contact a business too. Without structure, this will happen at different times of the year,
without a congruent message landing in short succession. Prospecting randomly is the fast track to awful results. Momentum
never builds for us or in the companies we are prospecting
into, and it's very difficult to track where you are with the key
accounts you are focusing on.

In chapter 3, we defined what we want to achieve with our
prospecting. Desired outcomes are measurable changes that
are specific and precise. You need a shared road map to execute
with your prospecting team to reach your desired outcome. A
structured outbound plan means that all resources are rowing
in the same direction, with key prospect accounts receiving
multiple contacts again and again. A mutual prospecting plan
will get your product or services in front of the executive team
via numerous individual messages, each focused on certain
aspects of their desired outcomes. By sending multiple coordinated messages, you activate the Reticular Activation System
(RAS) of key executives: the system that, for example, causes
you to notice Teslas everywhere if you're thinking of buying
one. Their subconscious works on your behalf. In the executives'
meetings, catch-ups, and other casual conversations, you can
be sure they will mention that your business contacted them.
It could be later that day or later that year, but either way, a
consistent plan to prospect will end up with the business being

aware of your service. I have seen it culminate in a message like this from a CEO: "My executive team keeps saying that your solution can help us. When can we chat?" Still thinking of the Tesla? I bet you can't stop noticing Teslas over the next few days!

Without structure, you can't manage performance or learn how to get better. A possible obstacle to prospecting could be a lack of contacts or content for a personalized message. It's possible to gain clarity on the obstacles between you and your desired prospecting success. Having a prospecting road map will define possible obstacles so you can make plans to get past them. Once a prospecting road map is created, you can commit yourself to the tasks. Knowing what to do and when to do it makes prospecting much more effective. Prospecting actually becomes a pleasurable and rewarding activity when you connect your hard work to great results. Structured and disciplined prospecting following a plan is crucial. The more structured the prospecting plan, the more consistent the pipeline generation becomes.

Don't Get Lost in the Noise

Commonly faced obstacles include the lack of a list, providing little to no context for messages, and using no innovation when it comes to sending the messaging. Some prospects receive hundreds of messages every day, most of which don't resonate with a problem they are trying to solve. Other obstacles might include being unable to dedicate the time to send consistent volumes of cold outreach or not having the time to continually send high-quality messages. Do you have a framework for crafting messages and a considered cadence for sending messages, and if someone is helping with the cold outreach, are they on the same page as you?

To ensure you stick to your committed outreach, could you spend time with an accountability partner, like a fellow sales professional? You could even ask your leadership to hold you to account.

**How will prospects you send cold outreach
to progress to their desired outcome?**

- What are the possible obstacles for the prospect to respond to cold outreach?

**How will you progress your
desired outcome of cold outreach?**

- What are your possible obstacles for cold outreach?

- What is the shared road map (internal) for cold-outreach activities? Who is sending what, and when?

- How will you confirm commitment for your cold-outreach activities? And colleagues' activities, if they have committed to helping?

Communicating Progress

It's no surprise that there are many obstacles to progressing a qualification call. Are you speaking with the decision maker? Can whoever else needs to be involved in the decision be included in the next session? What is the business outcome the prospect is aspiring toward? How will the budget be justified? What makes solving this problem a priority? How much is it worth to the business?

You can look to overcome these obstacles by communicating in advance what will improve the outcome of the call for them.

This can include relevant information required to qualify the opportunity, like budget and specifics of the current state, and this sometimes kick-starts the prospect's plan to get someone else involved. If you use partners to implement your services, you could mitigate an obstacle for the prospect by including them early in the shared road map.

Confirming commitment with prospects is difficult. We find it's better to over-communicate than under-communicate, so contact prior to and after the qualification call is a great way to get and maintain commitment for the next steps.

How will prospects on qualification calls progress to their desired outcome?

- What are the possible obstacles for prospects on qualification calls?

- How will you agree on mutual next steps with the prospect?

- What commitments will they want from you?

How will you progress prospects on qualification calls to your desired outcome?

- What are the possible obstacles to the deal being qualified? What can you do in advance to mitigate the obstacles?

- If you qualify the prospect, how will you agree on a shared road map for an evaluation with them?

- How will you gain further commitment from the prospect (e.g., get more of their people involved, or book in two or three future sessions ahead of time)?

**Are key stakeholders required to progress the
qualification call to the desired outcome? Or are
they required at a later stage of the deal?**

- What possible obstacles will key stakeholders present for
  the qualification call or later in the sales cycle?

- Typically, what commitment is needed from your prospect
  to involve key stakeholders?

- How do the best performers in your business or industry
  involve wider stakeholders?

Give Kudos Generously

Of all aspects of sales, prospecting is perhaps the most
important for momentum. It's important to know the possible obstacles to prospecting and how you can mitigate them.
Do you lack the resources to deliver a prospecting campaign?
Do you lack the time to complete the follow-up? Are prospects
receiving too much generic sales and marketing info to merit a
response? Does leadership track the success and effectiveness
of prospecting campaigns?

Setting a prospecting plan with clear instructions on who
does what and when, and reporting the success of the campaign internally, is a great way to stay on track. It can be used
to confirm commitment for prospecting plans from contribu-
tors in sales development, marketing, and other areas. Sharing
updates with leadership and getting team members recognized
and rewarded can also serve as motivation to stick with the
plan. The momentum of success will also help mitigate obstacles as they appear.

How will you track and progress
the prospecting campaign plan?

- Are you following a proven approach for what you are trying to achieve?

- What are the key milestones for this from beginning to end?

- Is there an accountability partner or team who can be responsible for ensuring that progress to each milestone is tracked throughout?

- What potential obstacles do you anticipate, and how will you progress if you run into them?

How will targeted prospects
progress to their desired outcome?

- What are the common obstacles that prospects face?

- How are they intending to reach their desired state without you?

- For prospecting campaigns, what commitment is typically requested by prospects before they agree to a call or an evaluation?

How will you progress your desired
outcome of the prospecting campaign?

- What are the possible obstacles to progressing the prospecting campaign?

- How will you get prospects to show commitment to evaluating your platform?

**How will you utilize key stakeholders to progress
the desired outcome of the prospecting campaign?**

- What are prospects' possible obstacles to engaging with key
  stakeholders?

- What are the possible obstacles to leveraging your leadership connections into prospect companies?

Committed Planning Pays Off

A plan is essential for sales professionals because it makes
deals happen. Running a sales cycle without a plan can cause
you to lose control of the deal. This filters down to the sales
meetings too. Planning meetings with the aim of securing
commitment to next steps stops you from losing control of
the meeting. Planning means you get all the right stakeholders in the key sessions and are less likely to be asked to repeat
any sessions, such as live demos. A lack of a committed plan
between the sales professional and the prospect delays the
sales cycle, wastes time and resources, and makes it very difficult to forecast when the deal will close. When running sales
cycles, you don't need to follow the plan to the letter every time,
but deviations from the plan should be on purpose to increase
the chances of winning the business. The journey of achievement starts with something the prospect is looking to achieve
and finishes with a desired outcome. Problems come when
there isn't a shared road map and there's no confirmed commitment to take the prospect from what they want to achieve
to their desired outcome.

Having a repeatable sales cycle isn't enough for sales professionals to be successful. The problem is that sales cycles

become too familiar and breed complacency when sales professionals are determining how the prospect's evaluation is going.
There is a danger that when prospects are agreeing blindly to
step after step of the sales cycle, you might assume it means
they are on track to sign by a certain date, since they are at
a certain stage of the sales funnel. However, if the customer
does not know the plan, then how will they know when to sign?
The customer could be expecting to sign next year and not next
week, if you haven't clarified it with them.

A shared road map contains the commitment of both the
sales professionals and the prospect to what will happen and
when. This means their date to purchase is qualified and can
be forecasted to the business. A shared road map helps find
blockers for the deal and gives you the opportunity for further
upsell/cross-sell with the prospect. This greatly improves the
accuracy of forecasting, which is good for the business and
from a personal perspective because knowing when the deal
will close means you can plan other deals or campaigns to
close at the same time to increase earnings by exceeding quota
and reaching commission accelerators to get paid even more.
It makes it that much more real for the prospect and sparks
thinking about how they will get this over the line internally
and how the project will help them make their company better.
And it will help you close more deals faster and earn you more
commission. Commission feeds your personal motivation to
get more done in less time, something all organizations are
striving for too.

Committing to having an annual sales plan, similar to
committing to a shared road map with a prospect, gives sales
professionals insight into how to achieve the annual sales number. Looking at the number as a whole can be daunting, but
having a structured plan for prospecting and selling makes it
easier to start executing and move beyond analysis paralysis.

Sell the Next Meeting

One of the biggest obstacles to sales meetings with prospects is a lack of understanding of the outcome of the session. Sharing an agenda, reconfirming the agenda at the beginning, and stating the possible outcomes of the sales meeting go a long way. An email ahead of time, sharing the agenda and asking what the prospect wants to add, helps confirm what they are most interested in. Clarifying this at the beginning of the meeting could help you bypass further obstacles later in the meeting.

You could look to reconfirm the road map you are both working toward and emphasize the value of future planned sessions. Each session with a prospect is an opportunity to sell the value and importance of the next session. Elite sales professionals tend to share why that day's session is so important and then ask whether the prospect sees why the session was so valuable: "What did you like about today's session? Great! Well, the next session is important because [insert reason and outcome]." To sell the prospect on the value of your solution, you must sell them on the value of each step throughout your sales cycle. Every sales meeting gives you an opportunity to sell the next stage of the evaluation, with the cumulative outcome of more prospects completing your sales cycle and becoming customers. It's also worth remembering that you need to sell the next stage of the evaluation to your internal team too, if they are involved.

**How will prospects progress their
desired outcome in your sales meeting?**

- What are the prospects' possible obstacles to achieving their desired outcomes in your meeting?

- What do prospects want on the agenda in the sales meeting? Did you ask them ahead of time?

- What will the prospects want from you in the sales meeting? What will they want afterwards?

**How will you progress your
desired outcome of the sales meeting?**

- What are the obstacles you could encounter in the sales meeting?

- How will you get agreement to a mutual plan and hold the prospect to account?

- How will you confirm commitment for the next steps?

**How will you progress the desired outcome
of the sales meeting for everyone else?**

- What possible obstacles may absent key stakeholders present?

- What is the broader business road map? What impact does this have on the desired meeting outcome?

- What commitment is needed from other stakeholders at this point or later in the sales cycle?

Strong Relationships
Can Derail Shared Road Maps

There are many obstacles to progressing a sales cycle, and I'm
sure you have come across most. One obstacle could be not
having a shared road map of agreed meetings and milestones
for the sales cycle with the prospect, or you might have one,
but the prospect does not stick to it. The prospect may lack
the time or commitment to get key executives or stakeholders
involved. Building a strong relationship with a prospect may
cause you to overlook basic but important information, like
the objective of sales meetings, and you might gloss over the
shared road map instead of confirming it in the detail required.

**How will prospects progress to
their desired outcome of the sales cycle?**

- What are the prospects' possible obstacles in the sales cycle?

- What evaluation plan are they following?

- What commitment will the prospects want from you or your
  business?

**How will you progress your
desired outcome of the sales cycle?**

- What are your possible obstacles during the sales cycle?

- How will you get continual agreement and commitment to
  follow the mutual evaluation plan of the sales cycle?

**How will key stakeholders get involved and
progress the desired outcome of the sales cycle?**

- What possible obstacles will involving key stakeholders present for the prospect?

- For larger deals, can you involve a senior leader from your business early in the sales cycle to get them acquainted so that they can speak if the deal stalls?

Don't Forget Your Annual Sales Plan

The biggest obstacle to progressing your annual sales plan is forgetting to follow the plan once you become busy and get a few deals signed. Staying on top of tracking your plan's progress is one of the most important aspects of a successful annual sales plan. Are you creating a plan that will be forgotten, that's too ambitious, that lacks grounding in data, or that takes an unrealistic amount of time? How will you hold people accountable to their participation in your plan?

Do you have a section that clearly states what is required from each stakeholder you want help from? Do your colleagues and leadership agree to support your plan? Can you share it publicly to garner commitment? How will you keep extended team stakeholders updated on the progress of the annual sales plan? How will you keep them interested and excited?

How will you track and progress your sales attainment plan?

- What metrics will you track?

- What are the goals, key milestones, and key dates of your plan?

- Who is holding you accountable to your plan?

- What obstacles do you foresee?

- How will you progress this if you meet those obstacles?

How will stakeholders with a vested interest help progress the desired outcome of your sales attainment plan?

- How will colleagues and leaders help you with your plan?

- Can you ask a specific stakeholder to be your accountability partner to ensure you execute the plan?

Don't Go in Blind—and Don't Be Invisible

I'll bet you're surprised to hear the phrase "shared road map" in the context of job hunting. Seeking a new role, especially a promotion, without understanding what the hiring leader is looking for in the perfect candidate, what personal improvements you need to make, and what your pitch (story) deck should be for the interview is a mistake. The hiring leader is running a process to find the best candidate, so it's your responsibility to allow them to evaluate exactly what you can offer them. Remember, you are selling *you* to the hiring leader, just as you would a product or service!

Not having a shared road map for your promotion campaign means you won't have visibility with the hiring team, you won't receive insight on key challenges or requirements you'll need to meet, and you won't receive input from the hiring leader on what the interview panel wants to see in the final presentation.

Seeking promotion with a shared road map allows you to discover something you didn't know about the new role and be prepared for obstacles you will have to navigate. The more you know in advance of the interview, the stronger your message will be and the better position you'll be in to get the role. Being fully committed to your interview process with a shared road map will give you the confidence to have a successful interview. A strong shared road map for promotion means that you can garner support and gain small commitments along the way (e.g., a hiring leader agreeing to review your presentation ahead of time or an influencer agreeing to join your interview panel if they can). In the best cases, the interview panel will know what you'll say in the interview before you say it to them because you will have shared key messages of your promotion pitch in the meetings in advance, and you maybe even have mentors on the interview panel.

Persistence Is Admired

A big obstacle will be getting time in the hiring leader's calendar. You are in the unique position of trying to network to get a sales role, so you can demonstrate your skills of persistence from a prospecting perspective. Since there will be others involved in your interview decision, making the effort to know the chain of command and finding time in the diaries of those who influence the decision could go a long way.

Getting clear on the hiring leaders you want to network with is obvious, but it's something you can't overlook. Who are you leaving out that you really should be talking to? When you do get a chance to speak with hiring leaders, it can be useful to share your career road map—where you have been and where you want to go.

If a hiring leader or influencer agrees to meet you, review your planned interview approach, and do a follow-up meeting for further advice before your interview, then ask them if they can try to get on your interview panel. This is important; if they agree to a second meeting, book it in their calendar immediately, even if it's months in advance. Use this second meeting to show you have incorporated their advice into your planned interview approach, and again check if they have been able to get on your interview panel.

How will leaders progress networking with top talent?

- What are the possible obstacles for leaders when networking?

- What is the leader's road map for networking with candidates?

- What commitment will leaders want from candidates?

**How will you progress your desired
outcome when networking with leadership?**

- What are the possible obstacles for networking with leaders?

- How will you continue to try to network with leaders who don't respond immediately?

**How will you leverage key stakeholders to progress
networking and key messaging with leaders who are hiring?**

- How will you get stakeholders of influence to meet with you?

- How will you encourage them to recommend you to the team of leaders responsible for hiring?

Why You? In Thirty Seconds,
Three Minutes, and Thirty Minutes

Figuring out how to progress the interview to a successful out-come is really about considering what might prevent you from being successful. Some obstacles could be the interviewer not knowing you, having mutual connections but not having them recommend you, or the interviewer having any doubt about you really wanting the role. All activity in advance of the interview is a great way to show you want the position.

From the interviewer's perspective, perhaps there are too many candidates to see each as a real person and understand exactly what they will bring to the role. They may lack the time to research each candidate, and simply skim their CVs prior to the interview. How can you make yourself stand out?

Thinking about the road map plan of being successful in the interview, if you had a chance meeting with the hiring leader, could you get your message across in thirty seconds? If the hir-ing leader was impressed with the quick chat and invited you for a coffee to talk further, could you expand upon it for thirty minutes? Think about the following: Why should they hire you ahead of other candidates? Why are you ready for this position? Why should you be hired now and not next year? These three points are memorable, and you can expand on them in great depth. Stepping back into an interview setting, having shared the same message, you could have insightful follow-up planned that reiterates your value. It also makes sense to confirm their timelines and commitment to the next steps in the process. What accountability do they have? What accountability does HR have? What happens next?

**How will interviewers progress
their desired outcome of the interview?**

- What are the possible obstacles for the interviewer to avoid?

How will you progress your desired outcome of the interview?

- What are the possible obstacles for you in the interview?

- What questions can you prepare to impress the interview panel?

Voice Long-Term Career Goals

You may not want to admit it, but there are obstacles that could hinder your promotion—a lack of clarity, little or no time with key decision makers in advance, not having a recent big-deal story to share, and so on. Is your future ambition aligned with what the leaders want for you too (e.g., outlining a step into leadership after an agreed length of time in this role)?

Having a point of view on your next role, what is needed, and how you'll deliver it is essential.

How will you track and progress your promotion campaign?

- What is your road map for promotion, including key milestones? What leaders or influential stakeholders will you share it with?

- How will you identify your gaps for your next role, address your gaps, and tell the story of addressing them (e.g., gain these skills, shadow those sessions)?

- How will you maintain commitment to getting promoted?

- Who is your promotion accountability partner?

- There are always obstacles; what might they be? How will you get past them?

**How will leaders who are hiring
you progress their desired outcome?**

- What are leaders' typical road maps for finding a panel of people to consider for a role?

- What are the possible obstacles for leaders looking to hire?

- What commitment do candidates who apply for a role typically want from leaders?

**How will influential stakeholders help
you progress your campaign for promotion?**

- At what point will you engage stakeholders that hold influence over leaders who are hiring?

- What message will you ask them to share with leaders about you?

CHAPTER SUMMARY

- Proactively seek the obstacles to be overcome.

- Always tell people what you're working toward.

- Confirm that you and your prospect are working toward the same decision and signature date.

- Consistent prospecting makes your prospect see your solution everywhere.

- Publicly giving kudos motivates people to work with you.

- Always confirm the shared road map and sell the next meeting.

- Asking a colleague or leader to hold you accountable for your plan will make you much more likely to execute it.

Chapter Questions for Hidden Habit #5:
How Will You Progress the Desired Outcome?

Strategic Preparation:

- How will you overcome possible obstacles?
- How will you share a road map?
- How will you confirm commitment?

9

HIDDEN HABIT #6

How Will You Measure Success?

Paul M. Caffrey

A lonely victory is hardly a victory at all.

PHIL M. JONES

HORT TERM? Long term? Intangible?

Do you recall when you were ten months into your sales career? Ever think, *Sales is not for me*? A sales professional ten months in decided sales wasn't for him and resigned. Disheartened, he was having trouble finding a new job. One morning he went back to the office to pick up some personal items. The company president led the entire sales team into the meeting room he was in, and he couldn't leave without embarrassment, so he sat quietly and listened. Salesperson after salesperson stood up and spoke to the room, and it reinforced his decision to leave.

Finally the president, who'd had a great sales career and had worked his way up to his current lofty position, spoke. "Sales comes down to one thing: seeing people. A sales professional of ordinary ability who can see people every day will be successful."

This message encouraged our rookie to give it one more go. In the last two months of the financial year, he made more commission than he had in the previous ten months. He went on to have an exceptional sales career. So how did he turn it around?

He started measuring the success of his prospecting, sales meetings, and closed deals. The standard sales cycle took one or two meetings for a customer to sign. He noted that 70 percent of sales were made on the first meeting, 23 percent on the second, and just 7 percent on the third or later meeting. He realized that 50 percent of his time was spent going after the 7 percent! He decided to focus on closing customers on the first and second meetings and cut the rest loose. That alone doubled his closed revenue. He figured out how to measure success and as a result used his time more effectively. Continually measuring the success of prospecting, selling, and other key activities led to him achieving a one-in-three close rate, and his average deal size grew consistently.

I know what you're thinking: *I don't have the software to track this. My* CRM *doesn't give me this information.* Well, he didn't have the software either. This story is over a hundred years old! Frank Bettger shared it in his excellent book *How I Raised Myself from Failure to Success in Selling*, first published in 1947. The content of the book itself is a great example of selling an intangible asset with potential future benefit.

A bad day can happen. Measuring success prevents it from becoming a bad week that becomes a bad month and then a bad year. Knowing your numbers gives your sales performance a fair advantage.

Prospecting: A Self-Fulfilling Prophecy

When prospecting activities are not measured, sales professionals generally believe they have completed more activities than they actually have. Without short-term prospecting success measures, it's difficult to get anything but mediocre results. From a long-term perspective, without success metrics we don't know if our prospecting is working. We can't determine which messaging and prospecting approaches are effective and which are not. Further problems arise when prospecting efforts lack efficiency or suffer the uncertainty of success. Instead of objective measures being the foundation for what is working, prospecting is based on anecdotal evidence, opinions, and biased data. Without success metrics, we can't pursue excellence. When the effort of prospecting isn't connected to successful results, motivation fades and a gradual decline in outbound activity occurs. A lack of success from prospecting then becomes a self-fulfilling prophecy, and a decline in prospecting will lead to a decline in the pipeline.

Qualification calls often become missed opportunities to understand your prospect's success measures for their evaluation. Unfortunately, the primary objective of qualifying the prospect overshadows their success metrics, despite them being more important to get the deal closed. It's less likely that demos and commercial presentations will include the prospect's success metrics if they are not identified early in the evaluation. A great demo where functionality isn't directly linked to customer outcomes makes it more difficult to close the deal. Initial qualification calls are great opportunities to softly obtain success metrics. As an opportunity progresses, though, it becomes more and more difficult to clarify success measures with prospects because they see it as an attempt to craft a return on investment to be used as a means to justify higher commercials.

Prospecting campaigns often suffer if they focus more on proxy metrics than success measures. The number of attempts to reach a prospect, the follow-up cadence, and when the activities are completed can become the big thing. Success measures such as responses, qualified opportunities, and closed revenue get overlooked. Prospecting campaigns without success measures mean failure is tolerated, and there is no feedback loop to learn from and iterate for better results. A key point of iterating that is often missed is the quality of the messaging used for prospecting. A little more time spent on higher quality messages being sent to prospects can dramatically improve prospect response rates.

It's possible to add success measures to cold outreach such as connection request accepted and personalized email sent, follow-up calls in the short term, and, most importantly, qualified leads and closed business in the long term. Blocking time in your calendar for cold outreach will deliver more leads when you are clear on the success metrics and the quality of the underlying activities. This means more prospects will be contacted with better messaging more often. You can test your messaging by sending one message to one set of customers and a different version to the other set of customers to see which messaging gets the higher response rate. You can also try sending prospecting messages at alternate times or in different formats (e.g., email, voice message, and video) to improve the effectiveness of your cold outreach.

Having a clear point of view on the areas in which your service brings value to customers is essential. On prospect calls, you can establish if your service can improve the same areas, then go a step further and try to quantify that. For example, perhaps your service removes a manual task for customers, and the manual hours can be quantified, with a value put against them to form the basis of an early return on investment if they purchase your service. You may need to do more work, but the earlier this starts, the greater the possibility of both sides pulling in the same direction to prove value. This will put better leads into your pipeline. If your qualification calls include success measures for the prospect early, they are more likely to complete the evaluation, increasing the chances of the deal closing.

You can also run prospecting campaigns that consistently generate leads, since clear success measures remove the guess-work. For example, you can determine which specific messaging is working with a certain persona a certain percentage of the time, and then you can objectively prioritize the results for current and future prospecting campaigns. The payoff is an ever-improving source of leads that increase in quality and quantity over time as each aspect of prospecting is improved in line with success measures.

Define Success

Short-term success for cold outreach could be simply getting a reply, getting X number of messages sent, or learning from negative responses why prospects are not interested.

Longer-term success for cold outreach could be finding messages or patterns that produce leads, improving messaging to better speak to prospects' requirements, or even building a more rounded industry point of view.

Intangible success for cold outreach could be getting better with the technology and getting faster at crafting the messaging.

How will prospects measure the success of cold outreach?

- How will you measure short-term success for your prospect?

- How will your prospect gain intangible success?

How will you measure the success of cold outreach?

- How will you measure the short-term success of outreach for yourself?

- How about measuring long-term success?

- How will you track any intangible (immeasurable) success you achieve?

Qualifying Deals Out Is Also Success

Short-term success for qualification calls can range from gathering intelligence to determine when might be the right time to move the prospect into your sales cycle to confirming they are just not a fit for your product. Success for prospects is understanding if you can help them solve their problems or achieve their goals faster.

Longer-term success from a qualification call could be getting agreement on whom to include in the evaluation and when. It could also be getting the prospect to complete an evaluation or even become a customer.

Intangible success measures could be improving your persuasive conversation skills and learning the questions and language that resonate with prospects versus what does not.

**How will prospects measure
success during qualification calls?**

- Again, think short term, long term, and intangible.

How will you measure success for the qualification call?

- And again think about short-term, long-term, and intangible success.

You Can't Manage What You Don't Measure

Measuring the success of prospecting campaigns is typically overlooked, but it's one of the few actions you can implement right now. How many prospects will you contact? How many outbound touches will you make? How many leads will you generate?

Does the prospect realize they can do something better? How many qualified leads reach your business's pipeline?

How many deals sign off the back of a campaign? Do you develop a repeatable process that finds leads that convert into opportunities? Do prospects get better results with your service and recommend you? Do you master how to run a multi-touch campaign that drives results? Do prospects get a better experience for their employees and customers with your service?

**How will you measure success for
your prospecting campaign?**

- How is short-term success measured for you? How about long-term success?

- How will intangible success you achieve be captured?

**How will success metrics and
outcomes be measured to define success?**

- What are the key performance indicators for your success metrics? When will the project be assessed as a success or failure?

- What impact will success have on your long-term goals and objectives?

- What intangible success is related to your overarching goals?

**Most importantly, how will
targeted prospects measure success?**

- What business objectives or company initiatives could your solution align with personally for the prospect?

- What skills or experience can the prospect gain from the project?

- What impact does success or failure of this project have on the prospect?

Establish the Value and Sell the Outcome

Again and again in sales meetings, we hear prospects say they don't need a return on investment (ROI) or a success measure to justify placing an order. The short-term advantage is less work; the long-term problem is that the later we are in the sales cycle, the more difficult it is to understand how the prospect will measure success, let alone calculate the ROI. The problem is exacerbated when our champion takes the proposal internally to get sign-off approval from the CEO, CFO, or sometimes the board, without clear measures of success. Sales meetings without success measures make it more difficult to progress the opportunity to the next stage. Fewer deals progressing through the pipeline means less business will close. The longer-term ramifications for the prospect who overlooks success measures is that they'll find it more difficult to articulate the value of a project internally for sign-off.

Success measures can be a bit of an afterthought in the sales cycle. Prospects view them as a tool to make commercial presentations appear more palatable. Chasing measures to show how the project will be successful and scrambling to create an ROI at the end of a sales cycle can become a bit of a mess. Prospects dislike it because it feels like it's to justify commercials rather than prove the value. This is a particularly strong feeling when, with so many opportunities to collect the metrics along the way, they were deemed not important, yet all of a sudden at the end of the sales process, they are! Sales professionals rarely track activities and calculate their ROI for deals versus the time and effort to close the deals. At face value, large deals are attractive, but if they come with an extended sales cycle that is much more resource- and time-consuming, the juice may not be worth the squeeze.

Annual sales plans are rarely executed, because they become a bloated wish list of potential deals with a range of vague activities to create pipeline and close business. They will include the goal to exceed the sales target, but they tend to become guesswork without any control or influence on performance. Annual sales plans are by their nature aspirational, so it's easy to create a plan around targets and overlook measures of success over the short term and long term. A lack of follow-through on the annual sales plan removes the strategic aspect of a sales professional's year. It becomes harder to take advantage of the opportunities in your world when you are operating on a tactical level.

Sales meetings are opportunities to mitigate risks to your deal progressing and closing. A great sales meeting has a clear agenda that is confirmed as valuable by the prospect and meets your short-term success measures. Every sales meeting improves the quality of your pipeline, but having clear success measures determines how much the pipeline actually improves. A sales meeting with specific success measures provides a more valuable experience, and at the end of it, you can be sure that you maximized the sales opportunity available to you. In a world of small margins, it feels good to give yourself a higher chance of progressing and closing more deals.

It's a great feeling to look at your opportunities and see them ordered by their likelihood to close. The better the success measures for each sales cycle, the more prospects will actually complete the sales cycle. Being able to call out that you'll focus on three opportunities this week (because as they have a higher chance of closing, for example) versus the other opportunities in your pipeline will give you and your sales leader reassurance that the maximum sales number achievable from your accounts will happen. Also, prospects in sales cycles with clear measures of success for the project have a better chance of getting sign-off because the focus shifts from their judgment of your proposal to the leading indicators for the success of the project, and how to surpass the success measure. It makes selling an idea internally that much easier for the prospect, regardless of whether they are trying to get approval to proceed from an executive, a director, or even a board.

It's possible to objectively prioritize annual sales plan tasks and close tactical deals, with a steady flow of average deals and while overseeing strategies that unlock large deals throughout the year. Being prepared to take advantage of career opportunities and building a network to open doors for promotion is within your control—no one else's. In sales, the right blend of success measures from short- and long-term perspectives improves effectiveness and provides more certainty. This approach creates more strategic opportunities that give the pleasure of providing more business value for your prospect with your solution, which means deals rely less on discounting to drive the close, but more on business outcomes, and the deals close at a higher monetary value.

Understanding and measuring success means that you'll take advantage of all the opportunities within your role. Sales meetings will be more valuable for you and the prospect, sales cycles will be more successful, and more value will be captured from the strategic opportunities you take.

Start on Time, End on Time, and Agree on Success Measures

Millions and millions of sales meetings happen every day, but the measure of success varies because rarely do you close a sale in a single meeting. A short-term measure of success for your meeting could be determining if the prospect reaches the next stage of your sales cycle. Prospects might use the sales meeting to establish whether you can solve their problem. Your business could view the meeting as a method to improve the accuracy of the business pipeline. Longer-term success might be determined based on whether prospects complete the sales cycle.

Intangible success from sales meetings is probably the most valuable to sales professionals, as the better you get at running sales meetings, the more successful you will become. Intangible success could be developing your soft skills to improve your discovery questions, becoming better at getting the prospect to commit, and making sure the next steps are always agreed upon, even if you are running out of time for the meeting.

How will prospects measure the success of the sales meeting?

- How is success in the short and long terms measured, and what intangible benefit might it give them?

How will you measure success for the sales meeting?

- How is success in the short and long terms measured, and is there the possibility of any intangible success?

Aim for Social Proof

A measure of short-term success could be getting the prospect to complete the sales cycle or the prospect signing a deal, while longer-term success could be the prospect giving you a personal recommendation on a professional social network or even becoming a case study on your website. Intangible success could be learning about the problems, trends, and specific language used by the prospect in their industry. Sharing these could help you connect with future prospects.

How will prospects measure success in the sales cycle?

- How is the short-term success of your prospect's sale cycle measured?

- How about long-term and intangible success?

How will you measure success in the sales cycle?

- Through the lenses of short-term, long-term, and intangible success?

If involved, how will influential stakeholders measure the success of sales cycles?

- Is it determining their team's ability to evaluate your product?

- Are they looking to make sure the evaluation team buys a solution that is fit for purpose over the long term too?

- Or is it something else? Are they simply looking to understand what you do?

Know Exactly What You Need to Do to Win

Measuring the effectiveness of your annual sales plan can be done on a monthly, quarterly, or even annual basis. Does the customer have more strategic engagements with you and your business? Do you exceed the annual sales quota? Do implementation partners close multiple pieces of business together and expand the customer portfolio for a particular subset of products?

A lot of important improvements are difficult, if not impossible, to measure. In terms of intangible measures of success, do you develop the leadership and strategic thinking required to deliver a successful annual sales plan? Do customers become better at evaluating and buying solutions that have a real business impact? Do other sales reps improve their sales skills as they close deal after successful deal?

**What impact and metrics decide if
your sales attainment plan is a success?**

- What measures will you set as your key performance indicators from short- and long-term perspectives?

- When will you check in and review the success of your sales attainment plan?

- What impact will success have on your long-term goals and objectives?

- What intangible success will you achieve?

Outcome-Based Networking
Will Get You Promoted

The desire for promotion often comes from the gut. You feel you want it, but you're not sure precisely why. We exchange our time for money, and our sales performance determines how much we earn. Networking with hiring leaders is great, but if you don't have ways to measure the success of the conversations, then you're just hoping they help you. Can you imagine meeting a prospect, not talking shop, and at the end of it just hoping they buy? It's difficult to get time to network with hiring leaders, and unfortunately, it's very easy to waste it. Some small talk leads to random conversations . . . and the time is up. You might even get the dreaded, "So, what did you want to ask me?" and have nothing meaningful to ask! Making connections with hiring leaders without success metrics that have clear asks makes it very difficult for the hiring leader to back you.

The success measures for interviews are generally assumed. It's not usually discussed, but hiring leaders have their own measures of success. Both sets of measures can be vague and can cause interviews to pull in two different directions. This can cause a lack of understanding on both sides and cause doubt to enter the room. There are few things more painful than leaving an interview and knowing the panel has doubts about you. Some people come in deeply confident and yet struggle to articulate their abilities. Their judgment of their own abilities can come across as overinflated and at odds with reality. A lot of people speak to the job description, not to the hiring leaders on the interview panel. However, it's possible to speak to your interview panel on an emotional level to trigger support for you ahead of others. Networking conversations in advance allow you to understand how the interviewing panel measures success. You can literally repeat the advice they gave you and some key phrases of language they used. This will let them know you listened to them and make them want to help you succeed.

Promotion campaigns tend to focus on short-term results and a few long-term tasks. Being ready for the next role means a lot has to go right. The skills, experience, and preparation can be overwhelming for candidates as they look at the next role. Promotion campaigns have clear outcomes to work toward, but often only the short-term goal is addressed: getting offered the new role. Longer-term measures of success, such as being successful in the role, are talked about at the interview but rarely acted upon in preparation.

The success measures of a new role and of the future position after this one will help you understand if you really want to go through the networking for promotion. It's also possible to network for the role after this role and state your intent well in advance. It's possible to be promoted twice in three years, and sometimes even more than that! As you may have guessed, the further you go in your career, the more evergreen promotion campaigns become. Taking a long-term view, it's possible to regularly exceed your sales target and be in position to promote, even in years you're not planning on it. Your success will lead to you getting a tap on the shoulder and being offered new, exciting opportunities. It's possible to navigate the career you want, adding year after year of exceptional results and useful experience.

It's easier for a hiring leader to take a chance on you if they understand what you'll bring to the role. It becomes less of a risk. Being aware enough to mitigate their hiring challenges works in your favor. By sharing this information about yourself, you're really showing you understand them and their challenges. The networking conversation is a tool to make you an "easy yes" to hire. It feels great going into an interview knowing the key challenges of the hiring leader and them knowing exactly the value you'll bring to the role. It is often overlooked, but showing how you measure success is important for all sales roles. The fundamentals will be similar across the board, and the detail will change, but understanding the importance of measuring success means you'll have no problem orchestrating it at any level. Ultimately you are showing that you will capture more value, discount less, and provide a larger contribution to the team sales target.

The payoff for networking with hiring leaders, measuring success for interviews, and running a promotion campaign is getting the role you want, faster! A calculated promotion campaign that measures success across the short and long terms and recognizes intangible benefits mitigates the risk of your interview going wrong, so you don't get overlooked for another year.

Make a Game Plan

Successful networking with hiring leaders can be measured in many different ways. In the short term, it could be getting a hiring leader to commit to being on your interview panel or being prepared to answer all interview questions. It could be getting the role in the long term. Intangible success could be understanding the hidden complexities of the promotion process.

How will leaders measure success when networking?

- How is short-term and long-term success measured, and how is intangible success recorded for networking leaders?

**How will you measure success
when networking with the leaders?**

- How is the short- and long-term success of networking with leaders measured by you?

- How will the intangible success you achieve by networking with leaders be tracked?

**How will influential stakeholders
measure success when networking?**

- How do influential stakeholders measure success in the short term?

- If you are successful in your new role, what measurable long-term success does that offer the influential stakeholder?

- What intangible success is there for the influential stakeholder (e.g., being known as someone with a network of top talent that can help their organization)?

Share Why You Failed and What You Did about It

The most obvious success measure is simply this: Did you get the job? Short-term success could be being able to answer all the questions in the interview. If you're not successful, then getting clear feedback on areas to improve is the secret weapon for your next interview. Sharing that you went for a role and were unsuccessful because of X, Y, or Z and demonstrating that you took the feedback seriously and did something to fill the gap is a huge plus. For example, perhaps the feedback was that you were too long-winded, so you hired a coach to teach you brevity.

Or maybe you don't have experience in management, so you took on a project that included managing people.

Intangible success could be getting experience in interviews and learning how to answer the tricky questions, learning how to read reactions, figuring out how to get your promotion story across effectively, and building empathy for the interviewers. Showing your excitement for the role and watching for triggers to see when the interviewers also get excited are difficult to measure but will have an immense impact on your future interview success.

How will interviewers measure success in the interview?

- How is the short-term and long-term success measured, and how is intangible success tracked for the interviewer?

How will you measure success in your interview?

- How is the short- and long-term success from the interview measured by you?

- How will the intangible success you achieve be captured?

How will influential stakeholders measure success in the interview?

- How is the short-term success for influential stakeholders who recommend you measured?

- How about long-term success measures and tracking intangible success?

The Position after the Position

Short-term success is being offered the role with the level of compensation you desire. Looking at the new position from the long-term perspective, what then becomes success? For most, it's getting an opportunity to learn (e.g., selling to a new customer segment or exceeding your targets and enjoying the compensation that comes along with that). Even on day one of a new position, it's important to know how long you intend to stay in the role, and it's also important to have a longer-term career path. Your next two or three roles can change along the way, but you should always be working toward the next position. As you go through the cycle a few times, you'll gain more confidence in making an impact faster and signposting your next position early. Ideally, your next position is called out in your interview for this position and shared with your new leadership team within the first few weeks of meeting them.

How will hiring leaders measure success?

- What are the short-term, long-term, and intangible opportunities?

How will you measure the success of your campaign for promotion?

- How is short-term success measured for you? Long-term success?

- How will intangible success you achieve be tracked?

- What will you measure along the way to show success before the promotion itself?

- How will you learn along the way?

Let's not forget the influential stakeholders:

**How will influential stakeholders
who recommend you measure success?**

- Yes, you guessed it—by measuring short-term and long-term success, and by tracking intangible benefits!

CHAPTER SUMMARY

- Not all success can be measured by a number, but all can be recorded.

- Sometimes success is disqualifying deals from your pipeline.

- Measuring your success gives benchmarks to iterate and improve upon.

- To help prospects measure success, connect the value of your solution to their desired outcomes.

- Successful meetings start on time, follow an agenda, have clear next steps agreed upon during the session, and end on time.

**Chapter Questions for Hidden Habit #6:
How Will You Measure Success?**

Strategic Preparation:

- How will you measure success in the short and long terms?
- How will you track intangible success?

10

What Now?

Paul M. Caffrey
and Phil M. Jones

Being naturally gifted is not the secret to success. **Being properly prepared and committed to action is.**

PHIL M. JONES

WHETHER YOU have a career in professional sales, are leading your own business, or are honored with the opportunity of getting the most out of others, this book has been designed to help you *think* before you act, with the objective of ensuring that every single action you take achieves a bigger impact as a result. It's about doing the job right, respecting other people and their time, and achieving levels of excellence by doing the basics, to a high standard, consistently. Using this book to amplify your own personal success requires just three simple ingredients:

- Relentless discipline
- A winner's mindset
- Non-negotiable habits

Discipline means you leave your ego behind and remind yourself that your experience is not as valuable as you think it is, and that even the world's greatest do their homework. A winner has the mindset that doing this work gives you a true competitive edge over others. These traits, plus the strength to know that these practices are something you should always do, are what compound into genuine elite performance.

Sure, you will find times when your work before the work is mere moments ahead of a new opportunity and takes just a handful of minutes. As well, there will be times when you rally your team to really research and think ahead of that next big presentation. In those cases, before entering into a discussion, you always ask:

- What am I looking to achieve?
- What is the current situation?
- What is the decision-making process?

And you always do what it takes to show them that you know them.

Then, in your discussions, you fuel your conversations with curiosity so that you consider:

- How will you achieve what's required?
- How will you progress the desired outcome?
- How will you measure success for all parties?

This is about taking full personal responsibility for the entire situation and understanding that your role is perhaps the most important role in each and every deal you are looking to make. Why? Because you are the one who sees the genuine opportunity, creates that opportunity, and then gains buy-in to make it a reality. Then you do what it takes to bring everybody with you through the journey, set clear expectations for all, and take full accountability for over-delivering on your promise, allowing other people to be the heroes.

The work before the work is always going to be work, and thankfully most of those you are competing with are just too lazy to do it. The fact that you have reached this point in the book is proof that you are already committed to realizing long-term success for your clients, your company, and yourself—helping set a new standard for what an elite sales professional really is.

The Work before the Work Assessment

How ready are you for your prospecting activities? How ready are you for your sales opportunities? How ready are you for your next career opportunity? Are you ready to set new standards for yourself and rise through the ranks to become elite? If you lead a team, how ready are they for the opportunities ahead?

I can hear you thinking, *I don't need to do an assessment. I have taken away the ideas and will apply them myself.* That is exactly why you need to take the assessment. How many times have you received excellent sales training and done nothing with it? Elite performers are proud of their ability to work hard, and they consciously make the decision to implement new learnings into their routines. We all know what we should do to become fit, to make more money, or to improve our network, but only a tiny percentage of us actually do it! What does this mean? Most people make the decision not to do what they know they should do.

The Work before the Work only works if you know your starting point.

The assessment stands between you being a good sales professional today and an elite sales professional quarter after quarter. It's not the most talented people who sell the most. It's the people taking action.

Can you really become an elite sales professional simply by taking the assessment? Can anything really have that big of an impact on your ability to sell? It absolutely can—you can be elite for a single sales call, a full sales cycle, or an entire year. The more you prepare, and the more it becomes a ritual, the better you will become.

The choice is yours: Continue to show up to each conversation with little to no preparation, or start being prepared for every opportunity that comes your way. The hard work will be done when nobody's looking, but the exceptional results and greatness you achieve with preparation will be showcased to the world as you accelerate your success and career.

The reality is that most people don't *use* what they spend time and money learning. Consider all the training, coaching, and books you have completed. How much learning did you actually build into your daily routine? I'm guessing you have implemented some of it, because if you got this far in this book, you're not "most people." You're most likely a person who is motivated and who takes action more than most. Excitement and motivation make people use what they have learned, but the packed schedule of sales professionals causes most of them to cast it aside and go back to their comfort zone.

Taking the assessment to determine where you are at is the first step to making your prospecting, selling, and promotion activities much more impactful. It will let you know where you are today and what needs to happen to improve the quality of your sales and bring you better outcomes, which will eventually take you to a very special place: that of an elite sales professional.

Consider the benefits of committing to do the work before the work. Imagine each sales call, sales meeting, and sales activity giving you the best possible outcome more often. Think of the business you will generate, the extra deals you will close, the mountains of commission you will earn, and the job offers that will come your way. Consistent application of what you've learned in *The Work before the Work* can help you become a high earner and beyond. Think about what that means for you and your family. Consider how getting better at sales could improve your life.

The assessment is the first step toward building relentless discipline, a winner's mindset, and the non-negotiable habits that will help you become an elite sales professional. It teaches you to make professional preparation your superpower—something as natural to you as drinking your hot brew of choice. It will help bring you the levels of sales success you aspire to achieve, improving your professional and personal life. Completing it will give you the opportunity to build the life you want. We often hear that we write our own paycheck in sales. Ritualizing the work before the work is like adding another zero to your commission payment!

It's time to fulfill your sales potential and create and close deals you never thought possible. On top of this, you're building the mindset required to have a lifelong career of successful selling. These skills will serve you well, even if you transition into leadership or become a founder.

The assessment determines where your professional preparation is today and what it will take for it to become a non-negotiable habit. Your confidence will soar, and your stress will reduce significantly, as you'll be ready to make the most of each opportunity. The feeling you get from knowing you're prepared for all that each day has to throw at you means you can open your laptop in the morning and feel at ease.

As you do the assessment and see the results, you'll likely be wondering what it would have done for you had you applied this professional preparation earlier; you'll wonder what your younger self would have achieved.

Boomerang!

The boomerang has just come back to us! And here it is, the link back to the start of the book. Back in chapter 1, did you send the email to three people, letting them know that you're reading this book and asking for their best sales/business book recommendation? Sending that message (if you did) likely contributed to you getting to this stage of the book, as it will have given you a sense of accountability to finish reading. You should be proud of making it this far.

To take this a step further and ritualize the work before the work, we recommend asking one or even all of those three people to become your accountability partner(s) when you complete the assessment. The reality is that most people know what they should do but don't bother doing it. Study after study has shown that an accountability partner can change all of that!

Access the Assessment

It's time for the rubber to meet the road. Put this book down, and go to paulcaffrey.com/work to access the assessment now.

Time to Put Your New Superpower to Use!

Congratulations on completing *The Work before the Work* assessment! You should feel so excited about your sales career—because you'll be generating more income than you ever thought possible. You'll be accelerating yourself toward your professional goals, and the extra earnings can really improve your personal life as well. Get yourself ready for a really fulfilling time ahead—this process will change your life! It will give you the confidence thousands of elite sales professionals have every day because they know what they want to achieve and how they're going to achieve it. This is your opportunity to become an inspiration and a role model to those around you. Finding more business, closing bigger deals, progressing your career faster—it's all within your grasp. And we will be cheering you on every step of the way!

CHAPTER SUMMARY

- *Think* before you act, and ensure that every action you take achieves a bigger impact.

- Amplify your own personal success with relentless discipline, a winner's mindset, and non-negotiable habits.

- Your experience is not as impactful as you think it is; even the world's greatest prepare in advance.

- Supercharge your preparation and take *The Work before the Work* assessment at paulcaffrey.com/work now.

Questions to ask yourself before entering a discussion:
- What am I looking to achieve?
- What is the current situation?
- What is the decision-making process?
- How will I achieve what's required?
- How will I progress the desired outcome?
- How will I measure success for all parties?

Don't forget to subtly captivate people you meet by showing you made the effort to understand what's important in their world in advance with prepared comments and questions.

It's your time to become elite.

This book boils down to the fact that preparation is an essential skill for success in sales, yet most people don't bother to prepare. The good news is that preparation is always work, and that will never change. That means if you master the art of preparation, it's a skill that will continue to give you a fair advantage throughout your career. Most lack the discipline to prepare, and others waste time researching due to the lack of a process. *The Work before the Work* has given you the framework to prepare for almost any situation in sales, gifting you the chance to execute to the best of your abilities. If you make the six habits of *The Work before the Work* non-negotiable, then you will be so much better prepared than most in nearly every situation that you will not believe the levels of success you will reach over the next twelve months and beyond. You will be working harder than everyone else, you will be more disciplined, you will add more value, you will react faster in key moments, and you will know what you want to achieve and how you will achieve it. When something inevitably goes wrong, you'll be better equipped to get it back on track. You'll be selling with confidence, with passion, and with the other person's best possible outcome at the core of what you are doing. Preparation may not come naturally, and that's okay; it's done when nobody's looking, and it's a skill you will improve over time. The more you commit to the six hidden habits of preparation to power the success of your clients, your company, and yourself, the more likely you are to release the elite sales professional hidden within you—the one who's itching to outperform the competition.

Acknowledgments

Paul: First, I want to thank *you*. I hope this book better prepares you for the opportunities coming your way and that you generate more business, close more deals, and get more from the time you invest in advancing your career.

Writing acknowledgments is difficult because so many salespeople, leaders, and customers have inspired, educated, and influenced me that there are simply too many people to thank. Anxiety creeps in, as I will inevitably forget to thank someone. (If that's you, my apologies!)

Writing this book for three years has been the hardest project I've taken on in my professional career, but it's been more enjoyable than I could have ever believed. It gave me the opportunity to reflect on my fourteen years in sales and deeply think about what makes some salespeople elite.

The Work before the Work would not have its name were it not for my coauthor, Phil M. Jones; it's no surprise that he knew *exactly what to say* when I shared the book idea with him. Phil, thanks for your guidance, mentorship, and insatiable appetite for making this book better and better. It's been an absolute pleasure to witness a master of his craft operating at the peak of his powers.

Thanks to my mentor, Chris Ducker, for your insights and for the incredible people you have brought into my world who taught me so much: Sue B. Zimmerman, Pat Flynn, Hal Elrod, Lewis Howes, Amy Landino, Azul Terronez, Neen James, Amy Porterfield, Joe Pulizzi, Amy Woods, Mike Michalowicz, and so many more, including Phil. Special mention to Todd Herman—your advice and coaching on performance, strategy, mindset, and execution is the best in the world.

Thanks to Marc Benioff. Salesforce is an incredible place to work, and your trailblazing leadership inspires everyone to live the values of trust, customer success, innovation, equality, and sustainability every day.

There are so many great leaders and people who have had a profound impact on me. I have been fortunate to work closely with some and from a distance with others. Thanks to all of them, including Julian Murray, Rishi Arya, Sandra Healy, Tony Di Carlo, Gary Dempsey, Áine Corcoran, Chris Voss, Barry McMahon, Michael Bungay Stanier, James Finglas, Beth Ayers, Conor O'Malley, Brian Murphy, Niall Brady, David Leitch, James Clear, Cecilia Garcia Freire, Paul Lawton, Richard McGuinness, Conor Gleeson, John Barrows, Lucy Mills, Ant Morse, David Dempsey, Jon Hill, and Richard Potter.

I've also been fortunate to work with so many great sales professionals. Thanks to all of you for the valuable lessons you have taught me over the years.

The incredible editorial and creative team at Page Two have been an absolute joy to work with: Trena White, Jenny Govier, Rony Ganon, Christine Lyseng Savage, Peter Cocking, Chris Brandt, and Steph VanderMeulen.

Dad, you were the first person I told when I decided to write this book, and it pains me that you never got to see it published. Thanks for teaching me what it means to be hard-working and a great father; we all miss you. To my mother, Caroline, thanks for giving my brother, Jason, and me everything as we were growing up. Those were great days.

I would like to thank Michael Cotter for the random business conversations, Joe Forgy for the motivation, Phil McGrath for the early days, Fergus Doyle for his sage advice, Martin Quinlan for the encouragement, and Alan Geoghegan for all the laughs.

Finally, to my beautiful, clever, amazing partner, Camila: This book would not exist without you. Your love, inspiration, and belief in me made this happen. I can't thank you enough for all the support you have given me. To our beautiful daughters: Amelie, your curiosity and kindness inspire me every day. Marina, our newborn, you are truly a blessing; your smiles, strength, and little voice complete our world.

About the Authors

Paul M. Caffrey is a master of sales preparation. Highly educated in the fields of science and business, Paul has spent the past fourteen years mastering his chosen craft—sales. An elite sales professional, Paul is trusted by some of the world's biggest brands and most innovative scale-up tech companies.

Phil M. Jones is a master of influence and persuasion. He is the author of the bestselling Exactly book series, with over a million copies sold; the producer of the "most listened to" nonfiction audiobook of all time (*Exactly What to Say*); and a trusted advisor for some of the world's biggest brands. He has been an entrepreneur since the age of fourteen.

Help One More Person Discover
The Work before the Work

Post an Amazon Review

Scan the QR code and leave a review or visit paulcaffrey.com/ work.

If you got some value from this book, then please take thirty seconds to write a two-to-three-sentence review on Amazon. These days, books are judged using the universal recognition of an Amazon review. Leaving a review costs you nothing, and it helps us out enormously. Our best possible outcome is two thousand or more reviews, and we simply can't do this without you.

Gift This Book

The Work before the Work can help everyone improve their sales performance. Do you have a colleague or friend who might benefit from this book? A mentor who might like to share it with their team? Do you know someone starting out in their career whom you want to help be successful? If there is one person whom you think would benefit from this book, gift them a copy. You never know the serendipitous outcome that a random act of kindness could bring your way. To gift this book, visit paulcaffrey.com/gift.

This book is also available as an audiobook.

Copies for Your Team or Organization

Would you like to order multiple copies of the book to share with your team or organization? Not only will you get a considerable discount, but we can look at changing the cover and/or examples to better suit your brand. Email now at books@paulcaffrey.com or visit paulcaffrey.com/bulk.

Team Training Sessions

Bringing the power of professional preparation to life for your sales teams in a live environment is a great way to amplify the success of your existing sales processes. It would be a privilege for us to help your team, with options available ranging from live, in-person, remote, or even prerecorded sessions. Email training@paulcaffrey.com or visit paulcaffrey.com/training.

Speaking Engagements

If you like the concepts in this book, why not share them more broadly with your event, audience, or team? Speaking engagements are customized to your exact requirements, ranging from keynotes with book bundles to completely individualized engagements that will help your team ritualize the work before the work to outperform the competition. Email speaking@paulcaffrey.com or visit paulcaffrey.com/speaking and we can set up a time to chat.

Mentorship and Coaching

If you've reached a point in your sales career where you feel a little stuck or you're struggling to secure your next promotion and believe working with an experienced mentor would help you reach your goals faster, then send a message to mentorship@paulcaffrey.com or visit paulcaffrey.com/mentorship.

Courses

Check out our excellent online courses to help you prospect better, sell more, and get promoted faster. Visit workbefore thework.com/courses.

Connect with Paul

I'm super excited to hear how you will use *The Work before the Work*. Let's chat on your platform of choice:

Start with my website: See paulcaffrey.com for my blog and other great resources.

Check out the website dedicated to this movement: workbeforethework.com

Send me an email: hello@paulcaffrey.com

Connect with me on LinkedIn for prospecting and sales tips: linkedin.com/in/paulcaffrey

Chat with me on Twitter: @paulmcaffrey

Get even more advice on prospecting, selling, and getting promoted on Instagram: @paulmcaffrey

Connect with Phil

See my random pictures on Instagram: @philmjonesuk

Read automated posts and impromptu rants on Twitter: @philmjonesuk

Connect for business chatter on LinkedIn: linkedin.com/in/philmjones

Gain free training resources on my Facebook page: facebook.com/philmjonessales

Check out my website: See philmjones.com for my blog and more cool stuff.

Exactly What to Say

The success or failure of almost every interaction is affected by the ability to choose the right words at the right time. Hard work, talent, and perfect timing can all have a great impact on your success—but without the ability to steer a conversation and create an agreeable outcome, your effort can be wasted. If you've ever found yourself lost for words, or have come away from a conversation without the result you are looking for, then what you need is *Exactly What to Say*.

Learn the Magic Words you need to know to establish that crucial trust connection—and get what more of you want. Phil M Jones's international bestseller will provide you with the skills you need to increase your confidence in conversation, and boost your success in all your endeavors.

Head to **philmjones.com** to add this guide to your trust arsenal.

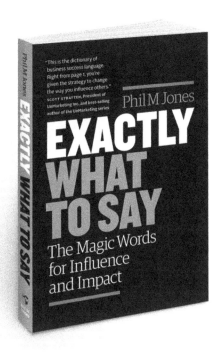

"This is the dictionary of business success language. Right from page 1, you're given the strategy to change the way you influence others."

SCOTT STRATTEN, president, UnMarketing Inc.; bestselling author of the UnMarketing series

CPSIA information can be obtained
at www.ICGtesting.com
Printed in the USA
LVHW021800310822
727260LV00003B/591